Raising Financially Fit Kids

Joline Godfrey

TEN SPEED PRESS
BERKELEY / TORONTO

Text copyright © 2003 by Joline Godfrey

A Kirsty Melville Book

Ten Speed Press
P.O. Box 7123
Berkeley, California 94707
www.tenspeed.com

Distributed in Australia by Simon and Schuster Australia, in Canada by Ten Speed Press
Canada, in New Zealand by Southern Publishers Group, in South Africa by Real Books,
and in the United Kingdom and Europe by Airlift Book Company.

Design by Pentagram
Photography by Jock McDonald
Developmental editing and copyediting by Melissa Stein

Library of Congress Cataloging-in-Publication Data
Godfrey, Joline.
    Raising financially fit kids / Joline Godfrey.
        p. cm.
    "Kristy Melville book" —T.p. verso.
    Includes index.
    ISBN 1-58008-536-9 (alk. paper)
        1. Children—Finance, Personal. 2. Teenagers—Finance, Personal.
        3. Saving and Investment. 4. Child rearing. I. Title.
    HG179.G627 2003
    332.024'054—dc21
                                        2003056416
First printing, 2003
Printed in China

1 2 3 4 5 6 7 8 9 10 — 07 06 05 04 03

To Inabeth Miller—educator, visionary.
Who, as a mentor, consistently made just one request:
"Dazzle me," she would say. And those of us who
were in the circle of her wise counsel would reach higher,
stretch farther, push closer to the edge to
meet her challenges to us. Her spirit soars.

Contents

Grace   ix

Foreword   xi

Introduction   1
It's Not Just About Money

Part One
Getting Started

Part Two
The Financial Apprenticeship

Part Three
Side Trips

Part Four
Map Check

Grace

An author enjoys the privilege of writing (and the agony as well—it is so satisfyingly difficult, I sometimes liken it to digging a trench with a shovel) because a cast of friends, colleagues, and smart people make the effort feasible.

This book is written in my voice and is a gathering of the things I have learned and uncovered while working with thousands of kids and parents over the last decade. It also echoes a team of people who have worked collaboratively with me for many years to experiment with, create, and design a new way to engage kids in their own financial development. Without the commitment of this gifted group of people, including Lynn Karlson, Barbara Dowd, Valjeanne Estes, Betsy Steiner, Jan Seufert, Michele Massman, Steve Simon, Christina Woo, Judie Framan, and Penny Paine, the book would not have come to fruition. The endless hours they dedicated to working directly with the next generation, their days spent searching for ever-more-effective and original solutions to old and universal challenges, have made my own knowledge deeper and wider. Together we have pursued a dream. Their strength and resourcefulness in the journey fortify me.

In addition, this book has a treasured cadre of advisors, colleagues, and supporters to whom I owe gratitude and tribute:

Kit Hinrichs, hero, inspiration, design genius (he'll blush), champion, and dear, dear friend, without whom this book literally would not exist.

Laura Scott, whose gift of realizing the vision of others is amazing; and Jon Schleuning, who is always right about everything!

Eva Miranda, whose vision for the book preceded my own and who simply would not let go of the refrain "You have to write this book."

Betsy Amster, an agent for excellence who always makes me better than I start out to be, and Kirsty Melville, a writer's publisher who "grokked" this book and was both advocate and contributor to the final vision. My real appreciation too to Windy Ferges and Melissa Stein, who were good-humored, patient, and instructive with me at every turn.

Melinda Little, who, with generous spirit of heart, shouldered even more responsibility than usual to make it possible for me to write this book.

Brooke Espinoza, Dia Rao, Kimberley Clouse, and Sarah Harden, whose insights and recollections added texture to my Persian carpet.

Joan Peters and Peter Passell, Carol and David Malnick, and Linda Hill and Roger Breitbart, whose love, support (material and psychic), intellect, and welcoming homes nourished (in a very real way) every page of this book.

Agnes Bourne, Fredi Stevenson, and Mary O'Connell, who each taught, encouraged, and cheered me with their wisdom and rich experience, and with whom I hope to have a great celebratory dinner.

Professor Howard Stevenson of the Harvard Business School, whose own work informed mine and who generously opened doors that would have otherwise remained closed.

W. Bruce Cameron, writer/humorist exemplar, who inspired my thinking on how to raise financially fit kids far more than the *Wall Street Journal* did.

Penny Stallings, comedienne/writer, who added wit and perspective when it was most needed.

James O'Toole, whose encouragement of my voice matters deeply to me— and whose comments on the book helped make that voice stronger.

Like my previous work, this book is built on the lives of real people. To the parents and children who taught me anything I know and have shared in these pages, a note of grace: From you came the simple lessons of raising financially fit kids embodied in these old, old words from Ecclesiastes: "a time to seek and a time to lose; a time to keep and a time to cast away; a time to rend and a time to sow…"

To you all, my love and thanks.

Foreword

Years before Alan Greenspan said "Improving basic financial education at the elementary and secondary school level can provide a foundation for financial literacy, helping younger people avoid poor decisions that can take years to overcome," Joline Godfrey was providing financial education to thousands of young adults. For over a decade, she has conducted hundreds of financial education workshops and summer camps for teens; in the process she realized that financial literacy is not just an issue for kids, but a family issue.

Broad economic forces, political shifts, personal needs, and societal pressures have now converged to create a world in which each of us has a personal responsibility to learn about and actively manage our financial lives—and to be conscious about the consequences of the financial decisions we make. Parents who have the financial bruises of the dot-com boom and bust; the loss in value of stocks and options, jobs, and insolvent corporate retirement plans; and mounting credit card debt, now want their kids to be armed with the protection of financial literacy. Fortunately the tools to make this possible are now more readily accessible. *Raising Financially Fit Kids* is just such an aid.

While the importance of financial literacy as a basic life skill has become obvious to educators and policymakers, how to develop this skill has remained a challenge. Schools, already struggling with insufficient resources to deal with a plethora of societal imperatives, simply aren't able to add one more life skill to the core curriculum. And parents, lacking confidence in their own financial literacy, often feel that the best they can do for their kids is to exhort them to save and to not spend so much money.

Raising Financially Fit Kids shows that such advice is not enough. But rather than simply reminding parents about what they should do, this book offers practical financial tools that do not require an MBA or a CPA's license to put to work—and that will work for your kids. Even better, Joline provides these tools in the context of a set of values and a point of view that reminds us that it's not just about the money. Rather, it's about raising kids with good values, good judgment, and confidence. In clear, understandable language, Joline provides the concrete and practical guidelines every family needs, and most importantly the information can be put into practice as soon as you read it. My advice: Read it and do it!

Howard H. Stevenson,
Sarofim-Rock Professor of Business Administration,
Senior Associate Dean, and Director of External Relations
Harvard University Graduate School of Business Administration

Introduction

It's Not Just About Money

I've worked with kids and parents in the realm of financial education for a dozen years, and in that time I've heard every kind of story.

- There was the mother who asked me, "What can I do? My 16-year-old is way over her limit on her Neiman Marcus card." (Can you say *scissors*?)
- A 14-year-old pulled me aside to say, "My parents won't stay out of my piggy bank. How can I get them to stop stealing from me?"
- A grandmother tells me her son is visiting the same bad financial habits upon his kids that she passed on to him. She wants to help her son teach her grandkids the right lessons, but doesn't want to hurt his feelings.
- A father confesses that where his teenage daughter is concerned, "It's easier to feed the tiger [fill her ATM account] than to take the time to instill sound financial habits in her. I'm concerned that I'll be sending her off to college unprepared for life."
- A very distinguished mother quietly whispers, "My husband and I cannot agree on how to raise our kids financially. We fight over this constantly."
- A father informs me his kids are "set for life" and has no idea how to instill financial discipline in kids who can and do have everything.

And then there was the following letter, sent by a young woman seeking admission to one of my company's business camps for teen women:

Knowing how to make money and keep it is not something people are born knowing. It is a skill that you must acquire whether or not it is from your parents, family, or friends. Money has always been an issue in my family. Neither of my parents own any credit cards and they are constantly complaining that they cannot get rid of their bad credit and must struggle to pay their taxes. My father has a new job every six months and my family has never been stable in regards to money. I've grown up always worrying about money. Somehow, it feels like others who may in actuality have less than me have more.

For the past eight years, my parents have been planning on buying a house. They never can because one of my parents is either out of work or we can't get a loan. I don't want to make the same mistakes my parents have made. I am now at a place where my parents cannot help me. When I ask them about the Dow Jones or the NASDAQ, they cannot explain it. When I ask my parents what a broker does, they don't have a real answer and they are embarrassed. I think I can bring my family and myself to a new level, but I need help. I want to learn how to make money and keep it. I think it is essential that I learn how to make smart investments and make my money grow.

This story and hundreds more are part of the driving force behind my work.

In 1992 I started a small project (originally called "An Income of Her Own") that grew up and became Independent Means, Inc., a company that offers financial education for parents and kids. Originally I created the company to give girls an economic head start. As I worked with the girls and their parents, I acquired knowledge that I began to see had relevance to all parents as they struggle to pass on solid financial values and habits to their children. With that knowledge has come a deep appreciation for the complexities of raising children who can function independently and who possess a sense of self and a strong moral compass. *Raising Financially Fit Kids* is my attempt to share what I've learned while observing, working with, and listening to kids who have been part of the Independent Means experience.

The children who have been my teachers are a diverse lot: kids from Manhattan and Minneapolis, San Francisco and Seattle; girls from the Cherokee Nation and Pueblo communities in New Mexico; Mexican, Australian, Brazilian, British, and French teenagers; and home-schooled, private school, and public school kids from around the world, both privileged and poor. They have taught me that kids are savvy and intuitive about the connections between money and independence, money and power, money and respect. They learn quickly that money is the deepest taboo, that it can tie their parents up in knots, and that—regardless of whether family resources are unlimited or in short supply—it is a powerful factor in family dynamics and relationships.

Not Just about Money

Raising Financially Fit Kids is not just about money. Rather, it is a book aimed at helping you launch great kids: independent, balanced, able to exercise good judgment, practice responsible habits, and live independent lives as contributing members of both family and community. That, I have learned, is what kids want for themselves. And if you, as a parent, didn't share those larger goals, financial habits wouldn't matter. You could just as well drop your kids like kitties in a litter and let them fend for themselves. But the fact is that you want them to live well and happily, gathering the skills that will enable them to make it on their own as well-rounded people. This book will help you achieve that goal.

This book is not about income level. As you will see, whether you have vast resources enabling you to establish trust funds for your kids, or you have a fixed income and struggle to make ends meet, the issues you confront with your children are often the same. This came home to me one day when I had a morning meeting with a Salvation Army captain to discuss how to make financial education available to homeless kids who participate in Salvation Army summer camps. Later that afternoon I met with the director of an organization that manages the philanthropic contributions of extremely affluent families. This organization was interested in programs to help parents raise sound kids in the midst of great wealth.

Teaching children to make ends meet and shepherd wealth are the concerns of *all* parents—and parental frustration over children who haven't mastered the habits of conservative spending and liberal saving cuts across race, class, culture, and political orientation.

This book is not about raising young tycoons, Nobel laureates in economics, or fledgling investment bankers. Nor is it about pushing kids toward a premature consciousness of material wealth. Rather, it is a means of helping parents walk the line between overprotecting kids from the real aspects of finance as a life skill and forcing them into an anxious preoccupation with money as a source of power and well-being.

And finally, this is not a book about parents as dummies. Or where you went wrong. Or what's wrong with your kids. Honestly, would you have picked up this book if you were a marginal parent or you really thought your kid was hopeless? Just as you needed lessons to play golf or tennis, or assistance from a tutor to help you become computer literate, you may need some help raising financially fit kids.

Financial Literacy Is Economic Self-Defense

Boom and bust markets, war and peace, health and illness, and marriage and divorce are just a few of the highs and lows that affect every life. Wise parents know that financially self-sufficient kids are less vulnerable to the vicissitudes of life. Every parent's deepest desire is that his children will never need to worry about where the next meal will come from or take jobs they hate "just for the money." And that instinct—protecting kids from the harsh realities of the economics of life—sometimes gets in the way of giving them the financial education they need. But financial literacy is economic self-defense.

This book will introduce you to the Ten Basic Money Skills, a list of tasks that collectively provide a primer of financial knowledge for your children. They offer a kind of armor to prepare your kids for life's challenges without scaring them to death. The activities in this book that teach your children the Ten Basic Money Skills increase in level of sophistication as the children mature. This incremental method of developing financial competency will help defuse the tensions and complexity of dealing with your kids around the issue of money.

The Ten Basic Money Skills

1. How to save

2. How to keep track of money

3. How to get paid what you are worth

4. How to spend wisely

5. How to talk about money

6. How to live a budget

7. How to invest

8. How to exercise the entrepreneurial spirit

9. How to handle credit

10. How to use money to change the world

Money and the Developmental Stages

Money struggles with kids are not an indication of failed parenting skills or financial ineptitude. Conflict that seems money-related often arises because, while Dr. Spock and his followers told us all about the developmental stages of childhood as they relate to motor skills, communications, and relationship capacity, these intellectual pioneers neglected to consider economic development as one of the basic developmental tasks of the child. That was a mistake, for personal economic growth is a lifelong process that has distinct stages not unrelated to the other developmental tasks of childhood. The following chart illustrates the stages that we all pass through in the course of our lives.

Key Stages of Financial Development

Stages	Responsibilities	Actions
Apprenticeship (5–18)	Develop financial vocabulary; establish early financial habits and values; practice saving, spending, earning, and philanthropy	Manage allowance; hold first job; begin community involvement
Starting Out (19–30)	Establish identity and independent lifestyle; experiment	Acquire education and/or life/career experiences; establish savings and a good credit record
Taking Charge (31–50)	Build assets; establish a foundation for self and/or family	Acquire assets; build career and family; explore life interests
Looking Ahead (51–65)	Take stock; mentor; contribute to next-generation needs	Reassess life choices/goals, and reenergize plans
Third Wave (66+)	Relinquish some responsibilities; plan for the next generation	Live and give creatively

You will see that I have highlighted the apprenticeship stage, ages 5 to 18. Do you remember anyone mentioning this stage to you? Probably not, which helps explain why, although 75 percent of parents think that providing financial guidance for their kids is a moral imperative, only 36 percent report having any clarity on how to do that. If you were left to muddle through the apprenticeship stage on your own as a young person, it may be difficult to figure out what good habits to teach your own kids—and how—early on in their lives.

My goal is to make the process of guiding your children through their apprenticeship fun, easy, and effective. Grown-ups who catch themselves thinking, "I missed my own financial apprenticeship altogether. I had to learn the hard way," will find that the stages and activities charts are so hands-on and experiential that, like Captain Kirk in a *Star Trek* time warp, you'll get a chance to relive and redo those years in a much more satisfying way.

What to Do If You're a Financial Novice Too

For some adults, part of the motivation to give kids a sound financial foundation is a personal awareness of what happens when you have not mastered money skills at an early age. If this is not your challenge, you can skip over this section. But if playing economic catch-up as an adult has affected your own financial self-confidence and increased your anxiety level, there are things you can do to move from novice to master while guiding the young people in your life through a successful financial apprenticeship:

- Don't beat yourself up. You aren't stupid; you just haven't completed your own apprenticeship yet. You can and will.
- Join your kids in their apprenticeship process. Remember this is about development, not chronological age. You can sharpen your own skills while accompanying your kids on their journey of discovery.
- Get clear on your own money values. Write them down. Focus.
- Get a money mentoring team for yourself. (See page 28 for a discussion of money mentoring.) Ask a group of close friends to help you on this journey. Be specific in expressing your needs. Spend time with them on whatever you need to do better: track your expenditures and balance a checkbook; save and calculate compound interest; manage debt and credit. If you need a brake on your spending habits, get a "personal trainer" to accompany you on shopping trips. Make sure the trainer knows your budget and is clear (because you have made it clear) what your wants and needs are.
- If necessary, meditate, do yoga, stretch, or breathe deeply before approaching money activities. Remember that anxiety can be a real brain and body stopper.
- Use money as another source of energy, not as a dark presence in your life. Money is the energy we use to fuel our dreams and manifest our values. As you read this book you will see that I rarely discuss money as an end in itself; I consider it a means of or a vehicle for achieving the authentically important things in our lives.

The Financial Apprenticeship Years

This book presents a different approach to kids and money than the typical "how to teach your children to save and spend intelligently" advice parents normally get. *Trying to reach kids on a purely rational, instructional level when it comes to money is a little like trying to feed them calcium and vitamin A instead of presenting food as a recreational, comforting, and delicious experience.* Just the facts, offered out of context with values, passion, and a sense of relevance (what does this really have to do with my life?) will not capture your child's attention at a time in her life when so many other things can seem so exciting.

Helping kids develop economic awareness is analogous to helping them develop good hygiene. "You learn to brush your teeth as a very little kid," I remind the teens I work with, "because it is a simple daily habit that most everyone accepts. If you don't take care of your teeth, you'll end up spending a lot of extra time in the dentist's chair. So, magically, you learn how to brush your teeth by the time you are 4 or 5 years old, and you think nothing of it. When in reality what happened is that you started out in a clumsy, awkward way, but by giving it a go every morning and every night, you got better quickly."

Talking, walking, and eating are the same: we start early and by watching others, making mistakes, and trying again and again, over time we get more skilled and sophisticated. We call this normal development. And we work at improving these skills for the rest of our lives—adult education classes of all kinds are advanced versions of what we start on as infants. While we take the developmental acquisition of motor and language skills for granted, we tend to forget that money skills are acquired in the same incremental fashion.

The Life/Money Map on the facing page offers a condensed visual explanation of this developmental process, both social/emotional and economic. This chart is the "skeleton" I follow throughout the book as I lay out a series of developmental tasks and activities to engage kids in their apprenticeship. You may use the chart to get a sense of what is reasonable and appropriate for your kids to know at the four different stages of development between the ages of 5 and 18.

The Life/Money Map		
Age/Stage	Social/Emotional Development	Appropriate Money Skills to Master
Stage One: 5–8	Is curious Has short attention span May have very high energy Begins to view fairness as important	Counts coins and bills Understands the value and purpose of money Learns to differentiate between wants and needs Begins to develop a sense of ethics
Stage Two: 9–12	Growing fast, body is changing Feels self-conscious Begins self-expression and independence Developing social conscience Becoming aware of hobbies and careers Strongly identifies with peer groups	Can make change Shows initiating behavior and entrepreneurial spirit Shows awareness of cost of things Shows awareness of earned money Can balance checkbook and keep up with savings account
Stage Three: 13–15	Focuses primarily on the present; has only a vague sense of the future Egocentric, self-conscious, and anxious about personal behavior Begins to think independently Conforms to peer group norms and behaviors Highly experimental phase; tries on different roles	Can shop comparatively Understands time-money relationship Begins to earn money; initiates small ventures Commits to saving goals Has basic understanding of investment Connects money and future Understands philanthropy Can read bank statement Understands interest and dividends
Stage Four: 16–18	Has increased capacity for logical thought and planning Preoccupied with acceptance by peer group Experimenting with independence Confronts serious decisions about life	Actively saves, spends, invests Connects goals and saving Experiences responsibility for others and self Able to talk about money and plan future Understands money as power Can read a paycheck, do simple tax forms Shows developing capacity for economic self-sufficiency

A number of parents ask what they can do with their kids before the age of 5 in terms of instilling financial awareness. "Lighten up" is generally my response. Your kids are absorbing a lot of information about the world; they don't have to get *everything* in the first five years. Obviously, tremendous learning happens for kids before the age of 5. But for the purpose of this book, we will focus attention on the years 5 to 18 as the apprenticeship stage.

How the Book Works

In Part One, "Getting Started," I offer insights about the dramas and challenges of raising financially fit kids. You will see that many of the family situations that appear to deal with money issues have at the root a mass of mixed messages and values that undermine the best intentions of every family, poor and privileged alike. Chapters 1 and 2 present a way for families to acknowledge and deal with the herd of unmentioned elephants in their living rooms.

Part Two, "The Financial Apprenticeship," gets down to business: this is the core of the book and the place where you'll find activities and suggestions for making the apprenticeship as much fun for your kids as a day at Disneyland (well, almost). Building on the Ten Basic Money Skills, each chapter addresses a separate stage of the apprenticeship years (5–8; 9–12; 13–15; and 16–18).

While reading the chapter specific to your child's age range, you can select activities that will help him or her acquire the ten skills, incrementally, over time. Along the way, you'll learn how other families have coped with the challenges of raising financially fit kids, and I'll tip you off to potential pit-falls as well as resources that will help you tailor the lessons of this book to your own family.

Let's assume for a minute you've come across this book when your child is 14 rather than when he was 6, and you're sure that he's currently clueless about money. Should you despair? No. Remember this is a *developmental*, not a chronological, approach to raising financially fit kids. If your child is chrono-logically a teen, but developmentally a Stage One apprentice with skills more akin to a 7- or 8-year-old's, go back and use those activities and resources as your starting place. You'll find that teens will cover ground pretty quickly, especially if you are clear about what these activities are and why you are pursuing them together.

It's also possible that your 10-year-old will be ready for the challenges of activities listed in the section for teens. Don't be afraid to follow his instincts. If you've been active about his apprenticeship early on, he may well be interested enough in what he's learning to want to speed up the process. Go for it! The Life/Money Map's "age/stage" designations are intended as guides for working with your children through time, not as a track that you can't get off.

Part Three, "Side Trips," covers a few special issues that may be relevant to your family. Chapter 7 explores gender-related economic pressures on both girls and boys. Chapter 8 takes a close look at raising children amidst affluence, a task that has its own set of challenges. How to raise young philanthropists at any level of family income is addressed in chapter 9, and chapter 10 is aimed at those parents with "adult children" who are showing no signs of developing financial independence and self-sufficiency.

Part Four, "Map Check," offers a quick overview of the most frequently asked questions about kids and money. In case of emergency, turn there first!

Throughout the book, I present a host of ideas, techniques, and activities you can try with your kids. Don't feel that you need to cover them all. Just choose those that seem to be the most applicable to your family—and the most fun.

Getting Started

"We carry our
homes within us, which
enables us to fly."

JOHN CAGE

From Safety Nets
to Self-Sufficiency

Families function as a child's safety net, but if you do not give that child the tools to knit his own net, so to speak, he may jump into a perilous world with no net at all. Helping children acquire the Ten Basic Money Skills is a process of helping them knit their own nets. As Federal Reserve Chairman Alan Greenspan put it in an April 2003 speech to a Jumpstart Coalition audience, "Improving basic financial education at the elementary and secondary school level can provide a foundation for financial literacy, helping younger people avoid poor financial decisions that can take years to overcome."

A Stone in the Pond

Acting on just a few of the practices suggested in this book will function like tossing a small stone into a pond: ripples will spread out in waves you cannot measure. So relax, have fun, and remember, anything you do is more than most kids get—and possibly a lot more than you got!

A dirty little secret in America is that the percentage of parents who practice the responsible financial habits they want their children to learn is appallingly small—and the picture is deteriorating. In 1999 the average household owed over $7,500. Just nine years earlier, in 1990, it was $3,000. Fifty-five percent of parents carry over credit card debt each month. Only 45 percent of parents stick to a budget and one in eight parents say they have nothing saved in a work-related retirement plan. So it's little wonder that, for many parents, the idea of becoming a money mentor for their kids is about as appealing as a cold sore.

But the fact remains that you have a chance to make your children's lives more secure. Where do you start? First, you'll need to take stock of:

- Your child's money style
- Your family's financial values
- Your readiness to commit to an experiential apprenticeship with your kids
- Your expectations for your children

The Money Style

What works in raising one of your kids may be useless for another. "My kids are completely different," I often hear from parents. "One wants to spend everything he gets as soon as he gets it. The other won't let go of a penny." Do any of these money styles remind you of your children?

The Hoarder

The hoarder. This is the child with a secret stash of money that she hoards assiduously. She may have no purpose other than knowing that the pile of money is there and wanting to watch it grow. The hoarder is a child who, when you suggest that she split the cost with you for the new toy she wants, will give up the toy rather than cut into her hoard.

Is this a problem? For the most part, kids who save in such a disciplined manner are to be rewarded (and after all, lots of parents long to see this quality in their kids). However, hoarding behavior can augur a focus on money for its own sake, which may hamper good money management down the road.

One teen told me about losing $200 she'd saved in her small change purse when she was 7 years old. "I just liked seeing and counting it," she recalled. This pleasure was interrupted one Sunday when, on taking the small purse to church, she somehow dropped it and never saw it again. Even so, it took her many years to be convinced that a bank was a better bet than her change purse!

Culture can sometimes have an impact on money styles and habits too. For example, kids who have moved with their families to the United States from countries in which banks have not historically been stable institutions may well exhibit the perfectly sane behavior of hoarders who know that banks are not the safest place to keep their money. Without making any rash assurances about the reliability of a banking system, if there exists a culturally based economic issue in your family, it is worth a serious discussion about how to deal with rational fears while making financial plans that work for the long term.

The Spendthrift

The spendthrift. The spendthrift gets a gift of money from Aunt Jane and can't wait to get to the mall to spend it. For this child money equals enjoyment, pleasure, self-indulgence. While the carpe diem nature of such a child is to be applauded, run amok it portends trouble with credit cards and debt. And if the spendthrift is the child of affluence, that brings its own set of complications (see chapter 8).

The Scrimper

The scrimper. The scrimper is the child who watches every penny and takes pleasure in saving, choosing less over more every time. A little different from the hoarder, this child will spend money but finds great satisfaction in coming home with money left over. The scrimper may find it hard to be self-indulgent down the road—and may have trouble being generous with others. In business, the scrimper may chronically under-resource projects and employees.

The Giver

The giver. The giver may be the kid in the neighborhood who organizes a car wash for charity. She may also be the one with a spirit of largesse who is always willing to lend her friends money when they go shopping. For the giver, generosity may be no problem, but attention to self may be a harder task. Givers sometimes have a hard time saving, as they can always see the yawning needs of others or may simply have a hard time saying no to the demands of others.

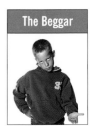

The Beggar

The beggar. This is the child with insatiable needs; he thrusts a hand out for something every time you go out. While this behavior is often the result of unintentional training on the part of the parents (always bringing home a gift for the least reason, reinforcing a steady state of expectation), it may also be a sign of a need that is not getting filled in some more vital way (attention, time, nurturing). This may be the child who feels most entitled and will face a rude awakening when eventually his tactic no longer works.

The Hustler

The hustler. This is the child who sees a "deal" in every transaction. An allowance may be just a starting point for this kid, who will try to double, triple, and leverage any financial gift or income in as many ways as possible. With all the signs of an accomplished negotiator, this child may be money savvy, but may need guidance to develop a moral compass related to his financial transactions.

The Oblivious

The oblivious. The oblivious child simply refuses to focus on money; "whatever" may be her most common response to your attempts to engage her in any sort of conversation related to money and responsibility. Intuiting that attention to this matter opens a Pandora's box of accountability, the oblivious child willfully resists practicing the Ten Basic Money Skills. This is the child who, if not required to become intentional about her money, will chronically abdicate financial responsibility to others.

With all due respect to Drs. Freud, Jung, and the like, there is no solid evidence that any of these traits can be blamed on Mom, Dad, DNA, or the excesses of the Baby Boom generation. Particularly when a hoarder, a hustler, and a giver live in the same family, it's hard to figure how kids pick up their money styles. Happily, whether you are dealing with a 6-year-old or a 16-year-old, a spendthrift or a compulsive saver, there are ways to engage each of them in his or her own financial education—but it will require the use of different tactics. In Part Two you can choose from a variety of activities that will help encourage financial consciousness and fitness. Some will work better with the oblivious, others will be perfect for your young hustler. And when the smoke clears, we hope kids will have grown up with a healthy dose of each of the qualities described above.

Family Financial Values

While it is true that some kids will develop profligate habits even with parents who are themselves the soul of cautious money management, you'll have greater standing to make demands and set expectations if your values about money are explicit in the family and if you are walking the talk. Mixed messages about family money values will make your child's apprenticeship more confusing than it needs to be. Take stock:

- Do you have a clear set of values about spending, investing, and giving money away?
- Do you caution your kids to spend wisely but carry debt on your credit cards each month?
- Do you urge your kids to be responsible but use money to "make problems go away"?
- Do you want your kids to know the difference between needs and wants but find yourself binge giving?
- Can you really "give your kids everything" but feel guilty or worried that unfettered indulgence may have unintended consequences?

My friend Sarah tells the story of her first summer employment when she was 14. Receiving in one lump sum the few hundred dollars she had earned, she took the money and promptly purchased a jacket she had had her eye on for weeks—one with a fancy leather collar. On arriving home with her new purchase, her mom sat her down and explained that had she waited till the jacket was on sale, invested the amount she had saved ($100 was the estimate they used), and added another $100 every year until she was 45, the money would have grown to almost $10,000, thanks to the power of compound interest. Sarah was duly impressed. But, she adds, her dad came home the next night with the matching pants.

Sarah laughs about this story today, but she also tells it to demonstrate the mixed messages her parents sent her. While Mom preached the virtues of sound buying decisions and saving, Dad indulged his daughter with an air of "Why wait? Live for the moment!"—not an uncommon dynamic in many homes. Of course, kids figure this out well before they hit kindergarten. They are savvy about which parent to ask for a treat—and they also intuit very quickly when a *no* from one parent may simply be a *maybe* from the other.

It's likely that any differing values will become apparent as you take a look at the multiple points of view that exist in your family (on pages 61–64 you'll find a few activities that will help you pinpoint these views and values). Mom may communicate that living beneath your means is the best course for one's life; Dad may be more inclined to take a chance to increase one's means. Uncle Ray may live from paycheck to paycheck while Grandma advises the family to take a long view about saving money and giving it away in philanthropic actions.

It's unlikely that members of any family will ever be in lockstep when it comes to their financial values. But it's important to acknowledge such disparities in a way that makes you a credible money mentor to your own kids. Whether you think of yourself as conservative or liberal, devoutly religious or aggressively agnostic is of less significance than that you understand the impact that your beliefs have on the values—and the behaviors related to money—that emerge in your family.

At the heart of this book lies a defined set of values:

M oney is a tool for achieving and maintaining independence. Saving is good; accumulation for its own sake is not. Spending is best done wisely and within one's means (though a bold purchase or investment may also be an act of wisdom); greed is not good. Giving generously is part of one's responsibility to the human family; shepherding wealth is an act of respect—to the past and the future. Money is an energy (not a commodity) that can be used for evil or for good.

One can master the Ten Basic Money Skills covered in this book and hold a different set of values; the important thing is to be aware of what those values are. Together, try creating your own family money creed. The conversations alone will do much to lift the family consciousness of money values.

The Experience Versus the Sermon

In many homes the harangue is the same:

"Do you think I'm made of money?"

"Money doesn't grow on trees."

"Can't you do anything but spend, spend, spend?"

"If you can't save, I'll take away your allowance."

No doubt you can add some old favorites of your own to this list. Teaching kids about money is often an exercise in giving commands, making rules, giving little (and sometimes endless) lectures. In a few homes this actually works. But in the age of extreme sports, interactive games, and virtual reality, experience rules. And your big competitors (Disney, raves, and reality TV, among others) know that. For most kids—indeed, adults too—experiential, interactive learning is more fun, more powerful, more engaging, and more effective than sitting through sermons.

This is borne out by the responses of kids who, when asked about the most helpful things their parents have done, respond with a story about some very practical action on the part of the parents. Brooke, for example, tells this story:

When I was 12, my parents sat me down one night and explained that they were no longer going to pay for my clothing or haircuts. At first I was a little shocked— I thought I had done something wrong. But then they explained that they were just trying to help me learn to budget. (Although the meeting did seem to coincide with an incident in which my mom, fed up with me wearing my socks outside without shoes, said she would never buy me socks again!)

They increased my monthly allowance, but not enough to support every item I desired. There was a gap between my needs and wants big enough that I had to fill it with my own money from babysitting.

My feelings of shock were quickly replaced by pride in my accomplishments. I was the only kid I knew who paid for her own haircuts. I thought it was cool. As soon as I could work, I began putting away half of every paycheck. By the time I was in college, I had a sizeable nest egg saved and was able to take a year off college to live in Spain. I've not quite lived up to those rigorous saving habits since, but I'm still proud that I put myself through college and paid for both of my cars on my own. Even when I wasn't executing so well in other areas of my life, I was always proud to pay my own way. And now, I know that for me it was and is important never to be dependent on a boyfriend/partner for money.

Remember, this parental intervention happened when Brooke was 12— right at the stage when clothes are vitally important to a young girl and a desire for independence is emerging. Her parents shifted from a monotonous lecture on spending too much on clothes to giving her a hands-on experience with managing her needs and wants.

Brooke's financial journey wasn't flawlessly smooth ever after (what journey is?), but she counts this learning experience as one of the great financial opportunities of her young life.

High Expectations

We should also give a nod of admiration to Brooke's parents. Sticking with a program to encourage financial responsibility requires a level of consistency and determination that kids will often do their best to derail. As a parent, your first instinct is to "take care of" your kids and to "make exceptions." In this case, Brooke's parents saw "taking care" as helping their daughter to stretch—a key part of instilling sound financial skills and values. They didn't "let up" down the road when she had performed well; indeed, the stakes got progressively higher over time. By the time she was old enough to buy her own car, she both expected to do that and was proud that she was able to do it.

Setting the bar high enough for kids to grow while not setting it so high that they check out, feeling overwhelmed and defeated before they begin, is a key part of the parental high-wire act. You will find the Life/Money Maps throughout this book helpful in this regard. But it's worth keeping in mind that a child's capability often does exceed his parents' expectations.

For a number of years now I've had the privilege of watching thousands of financial novices, young people with no real financial skills or knowledge, pass through our summer programs.* Most of the time they can't tell a balance sheet from a cotton sheet or a debit from a digit. For the first few days, as they discover they are expected to present a real business plan or a well-balanced portfolio as part of their graduation from the program, they appear a little dazed.

*For more information on Independent Means summer programs, visit www.independent means.com

But all around them, counselors, coaches, staff, and visiting mentors act as though this is a perfectly reasonable expectation. At no point does anyone say, "Of course, you're just teenagers; we don't *really* expect you to understand these ideas." Instead, the teenagers experience high-powered, successful people taking them seriously, asking them questions they expect them to answer, and sharing information they assume will be absorbed.

And indeed, two weeks later, when it's time for the teens to offer a presentation to an audience of parents, business leaders, and potential investors—they do. Often their presentations are far more inventive, sophisticated, and clear than those of older, supposedly more experienced entrepreneurs or investors.

This transformation is driven in part by the fact that the adults assume that the teenagers have the skills and ability to perform, and then they *hold them to that expectation.* Arguably there are a few advantages. Kids working with their peers have an incentive to "measure up." The counselors are smart and just a little older than the teens themselves. Accomplished twentysomethings with advanced degrees and experience, they are certifiably cool. And they have time to devote specifically to a few kids in a very intense way. Nevertheless, if these "cool counselors" didn't expect their young charges to perform, there would be no graduation presentations.

In part, our expectations are a function of a phenomenon that media companies have understood for some time: kids are older at a younger age these days. *Age compression* is such that little girls maturing early spurn Barbie by 7 or 8, give up their Girl Scout troops by 12, and are ready and eager to be taken seriously and stretched to grow when they are 13. And young men, hungry for something more than sports to test their prowess, see business as a proving ground they can experiment with at an ever-earlier age. Made evident in the clothes they wear, the music they respond to, and the people they view as role models, kids' early worldliness triggers a hunger for something more than the usual pap they are offered.

Anthropological researchers Douglas and Rebecca Bird, reporting in the 2002 Leakey Foundation Newsletter on their work on children's growth in Western Australia, observed that "children in general have the potential to become as successful as adults at all sorts of activities that don't require size and strength…They can learn very quickly if they have the need or incentive to do so."

Bard College president Leon Botstein, well known for acknowledging the competency of teenagers, advocates the elimination of high school. "High school," he said in a 1999 interview in the *Christian Science Monitor*, "never worked very well…We've got overripe young people confined in an artificial, age-segregated environment without sufficient employment or stimulation. Adolescence is the time when students could and should be excited about and engaged by the arts, music, books, ideas, and meaningful work—and yet that's not happening."

Botstein advocates that 16-year-olds begin four-year or community colleges, enter vocational training, or try their hand in the working world. "The important thing," he says, is that "they should be engaged in serious, meaningful activity that would be more connected both to real life and to adults of different ages than is the 'sealed-off' world of high school."

Botstein's ideas may seem radical by some standards, but he is addressing the issue of age compression in an urgent way. His deeper message is that taking kids seriously, expecting more from them earlier, is simply a recognition of who they are today: worldly though not yet wise; older at a younger age; full of unchanneled energy that still requires adult supervision and support. Kids need to learn financial skills before the stakes are really high—that is, when they are on their own.

Working through this book, you may be startled or made uneasy by the apparent sophistication of some of the expectations and suggested ideas. I encourage you to at least test the viability of some of our suggestions with your kids—the sense of respect that kids experience when adults express confidence in their maturing abilities, as well as the respect you will have for the kids yourself, is a rare gift.

Moving On

Now that you have a framework for launching your kids' financial apprenticeship, let's visit and vanquish some "money monsters" that may have an impact on your progress.

"If consumer society
has one Achilles heel…
it is that consumer
society doesn't make us
unbelievably happy."

BILL MCKIBBEN,
AMERICAN JOURNALIST

Outwitting the Money Monsters

Even if you are a model parent with a firm grasp of your own financial responsibilities, there are some daunting money monsters poised to challenge your authority as a money mentor —and intent on speeding your kids along the highway of spending and consuming. The top four money monsters are:

1. Time: For most families there is very little to spare.
2. Peers: The influence of your child's peers can be more powerful than that of family.
3. Media and marketing: With huge advertising budgets and competing agendas, companies may sabotage your best efforts, tempting kids into the vast bazaar of the material world.
4. Magical thinking: From the tooth fairy to ATMs that seem to spit money out for free to stories of magically turning straw into gold (think of Enron's notion of "virtual assets"), kids get mixed messages about the reality of money.

Money Monster I: Time

Let's face it, there is never enough time. Whether you have a staff of five or *are* a staff of five, if you're like most people, every day comes to its close with a list of unfinished "to dos." And even as this book encourages you to raise financially fit kids, hundreds of other books want you to pay attention to improving your kids' reading skills, being conscious of their physical fitness, or nurturing their musical talents. As a parent you are bombarded with enough "must-dos." My aim is to help you become a better money guide for your children while getting you to bed earlier.

Creating a Money Mentoring Team

One way to compensate for lack of time is to create a money mentoring team for your kids. You might think of this as your sanity network—this team will give support to both you and your kids. Your team should include friends, relatives, or acquaintances who:

- Are comfortable talking about and managing their own money
- Have some special expertise or unique knowledge that will be interesting to your kids
- Are willing to give your kids two to three days per year to have a chat over lunch or dinner, hang out at their place of work, do some other special activity with them, or just be available for money questions and advice
- You feel at ease and open with (otherwise they will not be a good sanity network for you)

Kids report that parents find it easier to discuss drugs and sex with them than money—which is to say that the conversations rarely happen. Building a money mentoring team is one way to get the subject on the table and into the real lives of your kids. You can create the team by reviewing people you know:

- Has your sister acquired a respectable nest egg?
- Do you have a friend who raises money for nonprofits and can talk about the world of philanthropy?
- Do you know anyone who works in mortgage loans or commercial credit? Ask this person to take your teenager to visit a house that is being sold and talk about how the mortgage process works.

- How about the parent you met at the last PTA meeting who mentioned she's in charge of making sure her company's benefits are "family friendly"? Why not ask her to talk to your child about what a family-friendly benefit is?
- Think about successful entrepreneurs you know—would they talk about their life choices with your kids? Can they talk about corporate life vs. the entrepreneurial life?

The idea is simply to find a group of people with whom you can barter time: ask them to spend a couple of days a year with your kids (a team of six can translate into twelve to eighteen days of money talk per year for your kids). Of course you will want to offer a service in return—maybe a gift certificate for a massage or a great bottle of wine would do the trick. This is a practical solution for spreading the work around and facing the fact that your life may not change sufficiently to uncover an extra half-day a week any time soon.

Every family will create a different team. You might organize your best friend, a grandparent, your investment advisor, maybe an aunt and a coworker all to be on the team. Your best friend might recruit her father, a coworker, a favorite teacher. Whatever the particular makeup, the idea is to create an extended family of money mentors who will, over time, reinforce key ideas and expectations, offer a steady stream of money-skill-building experiences, and take the pressure off you as the only source of your children's financial education. Think of your team as part of that "village" you need to raise a child.

Making the Team Work

One way to make the team effective is to make it formal. Talk with team members; be clear on the role you hope they will play in your children's lives. Give them a *Money Mentor's Kit* (a copy of *Raising Financially Fit Kids*, a short biography of your child, and a list of three to five key family money values) and a solid sense of what you hope they will focus on with your kids. But get their input too. A good money mentor may be inventive in ways you have not yet thought of—and sometimes he or she will be led by the specific interests of your kids. On the following page, there's a sample invitation for use with prospective team members.

Dear _____,

I'm recruiting a small group of friends and family to help me raise a financially fit child. You've come to mind because {you have a rapport with Simon; Bill and I respect the life choices you have made; your natural ability as a life teacher with kids is so evident; etc.}. I am/we are prepared to return the favor in some equivalent way if you will agree to join Simon's money mentoring team.

Let me bring you up to date on Simon, who is now 11 and in the fifth grade. He plays soccer and is a fair-to-good student. We're trying to be conscious about the money skills and values we help Simon develop so he will become an independent, financially responsible adult. We hope that an active team of caring role models and resources will have a collective impact that will serve him well in this process.

If you are willing to spend four to ten hours with Simon over the course of a year (a couple of afternoons or a Saturday morning, whatever works in your schedule), it would make a big contribution to his financial education. I've enclosed a Money Mentor's Kit that offers some ideas to get you started if you agree to accept this invitation. But please trust your own instincts as well. Whether it's a breakfast to discuss how you started your own career or suggestions on how to manage an allowance, we are inviting you to join our team because we think that Simon will benefit a great deal by spending a little time with you exploring the ways money relates to his independence.

Obviously such a commitment warrants a trade on our part. I know that you love the theatre. How about season tickets to the Great White Way Repertory Company? {Or an exquisite bottle of wine, or tickets to a baseball game, or...}

If this is agreeable, I will introduce the two of you and leave it to you to get started. I look forward to hearing from you soon.

Sincerely,
Cynthia A. Parent

As to the ways the mentor might spend time with your child, it will of course depend on the age of the child. But to alleviate any fears potential mentors may have that you are expecting a graduate-level day with your kids, suggest some activities offered in the following chapters, as well as a few of these:

- Go to lunch or breakfast and discuss how, when, and why (as well as why not) to buy things like cars and computers and DVD players and houses on credit.
- Have coffee (or ice cream) and share your own story of financial independence: how/why you started your company, chose your career, or selected the financial plan you now rely on.
- Spend time surfing the Web to view some cool financial sites together and talk about what they do and why they are important. (Suggestions for websites can be found in the Life/Money Maps in Part Two of this book.)
- Take the child along to observe and learn about a financial transaction (negotiating the purchase of a car or other capital expenditure, for example).
- Send the child a letter or email stating your thoughts or ideas about saving, spending, and giving money away.

Money Mentor's Kit
Raising Financially Fit Kids

Ten Basic Money Skills Bookmark

Biography of your child

List of three to five key family money values

The key point to make to your team of money mentors is that they are not expected to teach your kids *everything* about money and financial responsibility. Let them know you are confident that the simple experience of spending time with each of them will give your kids the opportunity to absorb, observe, and experience aspects of a financial life that will have cumulative positive effects.

Kimberley Clouse, one of the world's great aunts/money mentors, shared this story with me:

For Christmas I gave my niece an ATM bank {available through Amazon.com for about $30} to teach her that money doesn't just automatically appear when you go to the ATM—you have to actually deposit money to have money. After she received the gift, we talked about how it worked: if you have $30 in your ATM bank, and want to take out $10 to buy a doll, how much would you have left? She was learning simple math while discovering that the ATM was not a magical source of money, but a simple machine that functioned like a big calculator. This activity flowed wonderfully into more conversations about ways to earn the money to deposit in the ATM bank. I am trying to instill a consciousness of her own entrepreneurial spirit in our time together.

Another of my favorite birthday and Christmas gifts is a budget. It sounds a little strange, but she doesn't just get money to spend any way she likes, she also gets a money lesson—and believe me, she does not forget the gift or the lesson. The first time we did this I gave her $30 to spend—which she thought sounded like a lot! Until we went shopping and she realized how much most toys cost.

Aunts and uncles make great money mentor team members—their bond with the child is often deep enough so they are trusted, yet distant enough that they are experienced as "cool" in a way that parents rarely are.

Money Monster 2: Peers

"But Mooooommm, everyone has one."

"What's wrong with it? Everyone wears it this way."

"Come on, the whole class is going to…"

Do these whines sound familiar to you? The power of peers to influence your kids—for better and worse—is a reality to deal with, not ignore, when it comes to money issues. Judith Rich Harris, author of *The Nurture Assumption*, maintains that genes predispose children to develop a certain kind of personality, "but the environment can change them… not the environment their parents provide—but the outside-the-home environment, the environment they share with their peers." According to Harris, that effect starts as early as 3 years of age and can show up in nursery school. When *The Nurture Assumption* was published in 1998, it was greeted with skepticism—flying in the face, as it did, of the conventional wisdom that kids were most influenced by nature (genes) or nurture (parents).

Harris may not be the last word on what most influences children, but it is hard to argue about the effect of your children's friends on their behavior and attitudes. I was reminded of this fact by a parent who told me the following story:

Five-year-old Kari lost a tooth and, on the instruction of her grandmother, put it under her pillow. "The tooth fairy collects those things," the grandmother said, "and will give you something special in return." The next morning Kari looked under her pillow and, sure enough, there was a fresh $5 bill.

That afternoon Kari was playing with her friend Lesley and announced that the tooth fairy had brought her $5 the previous night. Lesley had recently lost a tooth too, but her tooth fairy had only left her $1. Lesley could already discern that she *had gotten a lesser deal than Kari and ran to her mom to demand why. Taken aback, the mom couldn't come up with a good explanation, but the next time Lesley lost a tooth, the tooth fairy had gotten the message and increased her contribution. Clearly, tooth fairies in the neighborhood realized they were dealing with some valuable teeth!*

Down the street, 4-year-old Linda's mom began to hear about the acts of the tooth fairy and decided things were getting out of hand when a fairy could set an inflated price on a baby tooth hardly big enough to see. After a call to Kari's grandmother and a little heart-to-heart with Lesley's mom and a few other parents, they all agreed to contract with just one tooth fairy—the one that gave only $1 for a tooth.

Moral of the story for kids: don't blab if you're lucky enough to get a generous tooth fairy! Moral of the story for parents: share the financial apprenticeship stage with other parents, discussing standards and values and dilemmas.

Parental isolation contributes to the power of peers—and financial anarchy among kids. When parents aren't talking to one another, kids rule. And as rites of passage become more elaborate and expensive (bar and bat mitzvahs, Sweet Sixteen parties, proms, and first cars), parents often succumb to what's easy, leaving kids in charge. And worldly though today's kids may be, they are not necessarily wise.

Never has it been easier for parents to create and use communication networks among themselves, breaking out of the parental isolation that is so harmful to their kids. Whether talking to parents of kids on your son's soccer team or checking in with parents in your daughter's sixth-grade class, you defuse the power of your kids' peer expectations by agreeing on a few basic behaviors you will enforce as *parent* peers. Being the first parent to speak up and say "I can't (or don't want to) spend $3,000 on my son's prom expenses or $50,000 on my daughter's bat mitzvah or $25,000 on a new car" may be tough—and not all parents will appreciate your efforts. But it just may be a strategy for developing a new financial consciousness among your child and his friends.

Another strategy to employ when dealing with the solidarity of your kids with their peers is to embrace and co-opt it, rather than fight it. Want to get a point across about saving or spending money? Turn it into a group experience—other kids may find you "cool," giving your own children permission to listen as well. For example: are you concerned that your 12-year-old is spending too much money on fast food every week? If the after-school gathering spot is a fast-food hangout and your daughter is worried she'll be left out if she doesn't show up, no amount of sermonizing on how she is wasting money on empty calories will be effective. Here are a few ways to engage your kids' friends without alienating your children:

Scavenger Hunt

Scavenger Hunt	
Rules	**Sample List**
1. Point of the game: be the team to spend the least money on the most imaginative solutions to the hunt.	Something you would need at a rock concert.
	An overnight bag for a trip to Paris.
	Down pillows for a bedridden aunt.
2. You have 90 minutes to find and document your solutions.	An electronic solution for listening to music.
	Ingredients for a picnic with four friends.
3. Be ready to defend your choices and give detailed info to the judges, who can give up to 10 points for each solution.	Something with which to entertain a 4-year-old.
	Something to help your big brother lose weight.
	An alarm clock that guarantees you will always wake up on time for class.
	A toy for a cat and a toy for a dog.
4. The team with the most points wins.	A birthday gift for a great teacher.

Whether we like it or not, going to the mall is twenty-first-century recreation. Lots of kids think of spending money as "what they do." Once again, exhorting them *not to* spend is less effective than helping them make that decision on their own. This Scavenger Hunt is designed to help them become conscious about how and where they spend money. It does require a little set-up time, but the payoff is worth it.

Ask your son or daughter and his or her best friend to each invite six to twelve kids for a Mall Scavenger Hunt. The day of the party, organize the kids into teams of three or four each and hand each team a Polaroid or digital camera (the idea is to have instant results), the Scavenger Hunt list, and $500 of play money (raid those old board games you haven't played in years, or purchase stacks of cash at a local toy store).

The aim of this Scavenger Hunt is to be the team that brings home photos of the most imaginative solutions for the least cost. Once the kids have their instructions, drive or send them (depending on their age) to the local mall. Give each group ninety minutes to collect photos of the items on its list and agree to meet at a specific time (points deducted if a team is late). Have them arrange their photos and defend their solutions to earn points. You can repeat this once a month, working up to a grand tournament. Both their skills and their innovation will increase over time.

Financial Film Festival

Like the Scavenger Hunt, the purpose of a Financial Film Festival is to engage your kids and their friends in an informed conversation about money, values, and dreams. Set it up as an after-school or weekend event: one movie each month with popcorn and one of your money mentor team members to discuss the movie with the kids. See sidebar for movie suggestions.

Questions worth posing for the films include:
- What does the story have to do with money?
- What money values do the characters portray? How do the characters reflect or stand at odds with your own values?
- What touched you in the story? What made you sad, angry, envious, joyful…?
- What lessons about money and people can you take from the film?
- How does the film connect to current events? To history? To the future?
- What do you wish you could tell the characters to do?

Financial Film Festival
Baby Boom
Boiler Room
Jerry Maguire
Tin Men
Liar's Poker
Mildred Pierce
Sweet Smell of Success
High Fidelity
Executive Suite
It's a Wonderful Life

Money Book Club

What you are really trying to do with your kids is instill a consciousness of financial responsibility they can tap into to do their own learning. A Money Book Club is one way to achieve that. Invite five or six parent/child teams (if you like, this can be structured as a father/son or mother/ daughter event) to meet once a month to discuss a book about money—see the sidebar for reading suggestions. Local authors are often happy to speak to book clubs, so if there is someone you'd like to interview in person, go ahead and call, email, or write.

Eat and Invest Money Club

Promise your children's friends food once a month and a chance to start their own portfolio and you won't have much trouble getting them to show up. They will likely be the ones pressing your own children to join! In the beginning—and depending on the resources of the group, this could be an ongoing strategy—run the sessions as simulations and have kids organize themselves in teams. Have each participant keep track of his investments in a notebook. At least one computer should be available to check how each investor (or team) is doing.

See page 114–115 for instructions on how to start an investment club for kids.

The Charity Café

Altruism begins to emerge in kids at an early stage. Helping them channel it and learn responsible philanthropy is easy to do with this activity. Ask your child and his or her best friend each to invite six friends for a night at the Charity Café. The idea is to have the kids redirect the money they would normally spend on a fast-food meal. With twelve kids giving $5 each, they'll have $60 to give away at each monthly Charity Café meeting. (Over time they will choose to save and give more in one place—but more on this in chapter 9.)

Animal Charities	Environmental Charities	Health Charities
Humane Society	Sierra Club	Blood Bank
Cat/Dog Spaying Fund	Land Conservancy	Children's Hospital
Pet Adoption Center	Recycling Fund	Cancer Fund for Children
Animal Hospital	Surfrider Foundation	Ronald McDonald House
Rescue Dog Foundation	Botanical Garden	Soup Kitchen

Set up the kitchen or living room with five or six big charity posters (see sample above): one for animals, one for the environment, one for health-related issues, one for homeless children, and one or two blank posters the kids can fill in themselves.

When the kids arrive, have them put their contributions in a Charity Café Bowl and fix a sandwich. Serve something simple (peanut butter and jelly or make-it-yourself subs) so more time and attention is spent on the idea of charity than on food. Invite the kids to take a look at the posters and think about which of the charities listed they would like to see their money donated to that evening.

Then get the party started. Organize the group into three teams of four kids each. Give each team fifteen minutes to designate two charities to donate to. Once the teams have chosen, have them describe how and why they made their selections. Give the full group time to discuss each team's choices and then ask them to vote again as a whole.

Once the choices have been narrowed to the two top vote-getters, suggest that the kids do a web search (if this is an option at your house) to get more information on each of the groups they've selected. Then have them do one last vote to select the charity that will receive that night's Charity Café contribution.

Finally, give each of the original teams an assignment: one team to take or send the money to the group selected; another team to select new charities to consider at the next Café meeting; another group to find and invite a philanthropist (you can help them with this by providing them with some suggestions and telephone numbers—or have each of the kids ask his or her parents to recommend a family friend who might be able to fill this role) to talk at your next meeting. The older the kids in the group, the faster you can cede control and management of the Charity Café to the kids themselves.

If the group gels and the kids stay involved, you'll find that they will become increasingly sophisticated about their choices. For now, you can think of the Charity Café as just one of the ways you can engage your own children by engaging their peers.

Money Monster 3: Media and Marketing

In his very sage book *Fatherhood*, Bill Cosby observes:

> "A parent quickly learns that no matter how much money you have, you will never be able to buy your kids everything they want. You can take a second mortgage on your house and buy what you think is the entire Snoopy line: Snoopy pajamas, Snoopy underpants, Snoopy linen, Snoopy shoelaces, Snoopy cologne, and Snoopy soap, but you will never have it all. And if Snoopy doesn't send you to the poorhouse, Calvin Klein will direct the trip. Calvin is the slick operator who sells your kids things for eighty-five dollars that cost seven at Sears."

And those slick operators get slicker every month. You probably saw it at some point (though it has already been replaced by something even snazzier by now): the TV ad that opened with a teenage boy planted in front of his computer in a bedroom littered with clothes and papers and CDs and dirty dishes. His mother stands in the doorway pleading with him, "Clean up this room!" Ignoring her, the boy flips the cover off a bottle of Sprite. His eyes gleam as the camera zooms in on a number printed inside the bottle cap and the voice-over blasts musically into a celebration of RocketCash, delivering the boy from the tedium of his mother.

RocketCash was one of the first of the so-called *near-currency* companies, originally conceived as a great way to create transactional income for dot-coms. A number of companies pioneered online deposit accounts that parents could use to make online shopping easy for their kids. First billing these accounts as a means of teaching money management to kids, and trying to sound high-minded, these dot-coms paired up with the nation's biggest retailers to find more hip ways to manage money right out of your pockets—using your kids as funnels.

Today RocketCash offers a kind of frequent-flyer reward system for buying things. Sprite, Nestlé, and over one hundred other retailers offer RocketCash points as incentives for your kids to spend money on *stuff*. In fairness to RocketCash, this is just one of literally thousands of promotions that offer ever more inventive invitations to your kids to spend, spend, spend.

On billboards, in the school cafeteria, on the Web, or at the local fast-food dive, *buy me, buy me* messages prevail. No parent has the resources to compete directly with the marketing budgets of Gap, Nike, Nintendo, and Revlon. Whether you're up against the latest Austin Powers–meets–Mickey D's campaign or a super-action flick pumping out Eminem's latest CD, imploring your kids not to spend so much money is, for the most part, an act of futility in the face of such raw power.

The good news is that, in addition to banding together with local parents to set standards, there are antidotes to the daily bombardment your kids are exposed to.

Teach kids to question television authorities

Actively watching television with your kids gives you a chance to offer a running quiz about the validity of claims made, motives behind programs and messages, and the nature of the images shown. You don't need to turn your 10-year-old into a jaded cynic to help him think critically about the kinds of messages fed to him on TV. If you handle the task with humor and a light hand, kids will soon sort out the real from the manipulative and make good decisions on their own.

Experiment with a currency of your own

While retailers have been creating their own currencies to coax money out of your kids' pockets, over two hundred communities around the U.S. have created local currencies (Madison Hours, Ithaca Hours, Maine Time Dollars) to create ways for neighbors and community members to trade and barter with one another—or, as they put it in Maine, to "encourage the exchange of service credits…among neighbors and friends."

Madison Hours, for example, was initiated in 1996 in Madison, Wisconsin, to spur sustainable, grassroots economic development. As Camy Mathy reported in *Yes* magazine, she has bought "custom sewing, a felt hat, a printer for my computer, and garden seedlings." In my own community of Ojai, California, a local bookstore, Bart's Books, lets me trade my old books for new ones. I have a running account, save space on my own bookshelves, and can always afford to "buy" new books. In Ojai, books function as a kind of alternative currency.

These alternative forms of money can help your kids understand the function of currency while giving them up-close and personal experiences using the currency in your community. For more information on community currencies, visit www.ithacahours.org, www.madisonhours.org, or www.mtdn.org.

Make parental connections on a large scale

That concerted effort on behalf of kids is possible is made evident by the force of such efforts as Mothers Against Drunk Driving, Million Mom March, and Dads and Daughters. You *can* equip kids to think for themselves about the messages coming at them. The most media-savvy generation in history, these kids do not buy everything they hear about. But they do need a clear set of values to power the internal compass they will use to make their own decisions about what's hot and what's not, what they need and what they don't. Think of these values as a kind of psychic armor your kids can use to defend themselves against the manipulations of the media.

Money Monster 4: Magical Thinking

Kids often get mixed messages about the easy availability of money. Not surprising, when you think about all of the fairy tales that connect gold and magic. Of course, we *want* the world of children to be magical and full of wonder. What can be better than the look of joy on a 4-year-old's face when she emerges in the morning having found money under her pillow in exchange for a tooth? It's the same look of wonder a 45-year-old might have if he found an extra grand lying in the front yard!

I'm not Scrooge, and I don't think it necessary to drain wonder from the lives of kids to make them financially responsible. However, it is important to be conscious of the messages we send, minimizing the connections we set up for them between wonder and awe and money. The next time the tooth fairy visits, put a small toy or a movie ticket under your child's pillow, or a note with a promise to read a favorite book or take her on a special adventure. Whenever possible, try to separate money from magic.

Another culprit is the ATM—when they are old enough to use it, make sure your children understand that they are dealing with real money, from a real source. Open an account with a deposit that includes some of their own money from savings or earnings, then walk them through the process of taking money out of the ATM, reading the account slip, and then calling the bank's toll-free number to confirm that their account balance has decreased. The greatest disservice a parent can do—even if you can well afford to—is to make a deposit, give your child an ATM card, and keep filling the well every time she runs out.

If you suspect that magical thinking about money is something kids "get over," think again. I once ran a seminar on kids and money for a group of private-school teachers. Going around the room, I asked each of the teachers to describe some of the key themes that came to mind when they thought of money. Two of the teachers in that room replied "magic" without batting an eyelash. As I pressed to learn more, they all talked about how nervous they were in dealing with money—still, as adults. By not thinking about money and by treating it as a "magical" element in their lives, they did not have to take responsibility for dealing with it.

Yet raising financially fit kids needn't be mysterious or overly taxing. If your goal is simply to raise a great kid (as opposed to, say, a teenage arbitrager), then a modicum of attention to the basics we have just covered—money styles, money values, and the money monsters you are in a contest with—is about all you need to guide your kids through a financial apprenticeship. Moreover, if you assemble a loving and reliable money mentoring team, you won't have to travel this journey alone.

In Part Two, "The Financial Apprenticeship," I'll offer specific how-to's for countering money monsters and keeping your kids focused on this most critical part of their quest for independence.

Resources to Help Kids Get Media Literate

The National Institute on Media and the Family, www.mediafamily.org

TV Smarts for Kids video, call (703) 845-1400 for free copy

Killing Us Softly III, a documentary on gender representation in advertising by Jean Kilbourne www.jeankilbourne.com

SNAPS: Photo Cards for Media Literacy, available through www.medialit.org

The Financial Apprenticeship

The Money Skills Map

I've pointed out some of the pressures your children face as they start out on their financial journey. The next four chapters will introduce you to the Ten Basic Money Skills that constitute the apprentice's financial tool kit, and will present activities tailored to four age groups between 5 and 18. This chart will be filled in chapter by chapter, offering specific activities for each age group and money skill. Selecting from the myriad activities will give you a personalized plan for your own family.

Ages 5–8:
I'm Just A Kid

Though your children will be appropriately preoccupied with many developmental tasks during these years, this is the stage when you find ways to introduce very basic money skills and values.

10 Basic Money Skills	Actions (5–8)
1. How to save	
2. How to keep track of money	
3. How to get paid what you are worth	
4. How to spend wisely	
5. How to talk about money	
6. How to live a budget	
7. How to invest	
8. How to exercise the entrepreneurial spirit	
9. How to handle credit	
10. How to use money to change the world	

Ages 9–12: Encouraging Passions	Ages 13–15: Breaking Away	Ages 16–18: Standing Tall
These are the years when you piggyback on all the unharnessed enthusiasm and curiosity of "tweens" to demonstrate the links between pursuing passions and having the means to realize those passions, and between opportunity and responsibility.	When it comes to money, these may be the most difficult as well as the most fun years. Children will be struggling to define themselves and will be taking the steps that lead to young adulthood. Behavior at this stage really does have consequences. In these years, true impact is possible.	These are the years when it all comes together or you are hustling to play catch-up. Either way, now is the time when acquiring financial responsibility can go hand in hand with a new maturity.
Actions (9–12)	**Actions (13–15)**	**Actions (16–18)**

"Someone's sitting in the shade today because someone planted a tree a long time ago."

WARREN BUFFETT,
BILLIONAIRE INVESTOR

Stage One
Ages 5–8: I'm Just a Kid

I once spoke to a group of financial advisors and asked them to describe some of the things they do to pass on good financial habits to their youngest children. There were a lot of great ideas, but most memorable was the dad who claimed he was teaching his 6-year-old to calculate the time value of money. I am of course all in favor of starting the financial apprenticeship early, but this may be overdoing it! Whatever money messages and skills you want to pass along to your kids must be done in the context of young attention spans and egocentrism.

Most 5-to-8-year-olds are curious, literal, and high-energy, and absorb information rapidly, shifting from subject to object to idea to experience in nanoseconds. How then to get them started on a journey of economic literacy that will last a lifetime?

The Life/Money Map
Stage One/Ages 5–8

Social / Emotional Development	Appropriate Money Skills to Master
Is curious	Counts coins and bills
Has short attention span	Understands the purpose of money
May have very high energy	Learns to differentiate between wants and needs
Begins to view fairness as important	Begins to develop a sense of ethics

How you live your life

is central to what you will teach

your kids about money.

7. How to invest	8. How to exercise the entrepreneurial spirit	9. How to handle credit	10. How to use money to change the world
Invest in the future of your children. Now may be the time to establish a 529 college savings plan for your kids' or grandkids' education. Be aware of fees that can add substantial costs to this investment vehicle. **Introduce the phrase** *compound interest* and show your child the numbers in her savings account passbook (on paper or online) to illustrate how money makes money over time. **Introduce the word** *equity* (ownership): "I'll be an equity partner with you in a lemonade stand." Explain to your child that you'll provide the money for sugar and lemons and he will contribute *sweat equity* (the hard work); that way you'll share equity in the business.	**Encourage entrepreneurial projects** (lemonade stands, baseball card stands). Help your child determine what to charge for products or services. **Praise your child** when she exercises her entrepreneurial muscle ("How enterprising!" "How resourceful!"). **Create a kitchen gallery** of young entrepreneurial role models	**Help your child get his first library card** and explain that borrowing books is a kind of credit card. You borrow a book, it is marked on your library card, you gain knowledge (instead of money), and if you don't take it back, you have to pay. **Let your child borrow small amounts of money from you;** make her pay it back from her allowance. (Be sure to use this activity to teach the basics of paying back debts, not getting in debt.) **If you buy something for your kid on your credit card, show him the bill** when it comes in and explain how you must pay for the item now, even if at the time you just handed a card to the store and it looked like nothing was happening.	**At Thanksgiving, allow your child to put cans of food into the food drive bins** (ask her to buy at least one of the cans with money from her "give away" fund). **At Christmas or Chanukah, make sure your child contributes** to a gift collection for kids who are in the hospital or who are homeless. **Create a family day** when everyone gives a half-day of volunteer work to a local nonprofit or community project.
Resources for 529 plans: www.savingforcollege.com *The Vanguard Plain Talk Guide* (free): (800) 716-4078 *Maisy Makes Lemonade,* Lucy Cousins *Once Upon a Company...: A True Story,* Wendy Anderson Halperin	*How the Second Grade Got $8,205.50 to Visit the Statue of Liberty,* Nathan Zimelman, et al. *Arthur's Funny Money,* Lillian Hoban *Uncle Jed's Barbershop,* Margaree King Mitchell Tips for creating a lemonade stand: www.bluesclues.net/lemonadestand.html	*Money of Your Own,* Grace Weinstein *Neale S. Godfrey's Ultimate Kids' Money Book,* Neale S. Godfrey	*Littlejim's Gift,* Gloria Houston *Sam and the Lucky Money,* Karen Chinn *The Giving Book, Vol. 1,* available through the Women's Fund: www.womensfund.com/GetInvolved/littleWomensFund.asp

Flip Open

3. How to get paid what you are worth	4. How to spend wisely	5. How to talk about money	6. How to live a budget
Post a list of "extra-credit" household jobs and a range of fees each job is worth. Once a week, each child must choose one job and negotiate a payment amount. Make sure it's clear that the harder the job, the more it's worth. (These should be special assignments; everyone in the family should pitch in to take care of everyday chores.) For these special projects, pay your child for his time rather than assign a flat fee. Make sure a time frame is agreed to ahead of time so he doesn't prolong the task to get paid extra!	**Next time there's a planned visit to a toy store** or other intriguing destination, discuss before you arrive how much money your child will have to spend. Set parameters for how this money can be spent, and discuss the choices to be made—will it be spent all on one thing, or on several smaller purchases? **Create a budget for pet care.** Ask your child to make choices to keep the total under a certain amount. **Give your child a calculator** when he shops with you so he can add the cost of purchases as you go. **Teach your child** to spell *discount*. **Be a model** of thoughtful spending habits	**Ask your child** to talk about all the ways money is used. **Discuss** what food drives and homeless shelters are for. **Never be afraid** to say "We can't afford it." **Never be afraid** to say "We can afford it, but this is not how I want to spend our money"— then be sure to explain why. **Set up** your first money-mentoring team	**Start an allowance program** (see page 50). **Give your kid a take-out menu** and a dollar amount and ask her to order dinner for the family without going over the budget. **Let your child live** with the consequences of exceeding his allowance or budget. **Teach your child** to spell *budget*.
Money-Savvy Kids, J. Raymond Albrektson *A Day's Work,* Eve Bunting *A Job for Jenny Archer,* Ellen Conford	*Annie's Pet,* Barbara Brenner Math Wiz toy, www.learningexpress.com *Alexander, Who Used to Be Rich Last Sunday,* Judith Viorst *Money Doesn't Grow on Trees: Teaching Your Kids the Value of a Buck,* Ellie Kay	*Pigs Will Be Pigs: Fun with Math and Money,* Amy Axelrod *The Monster Money Book,* Loreen Leedy *Money Troubles,* Bill Cosby *No More Frogs to Kiss: 99 Ways to Give Economic Power to Girls,* Joline Godfrey	Informative poll on allowances: www.familyeducation.com/ passion_poll/1,2286, 1-7661,00.html Site that helps kids learn about money: www.makingallowances.com *Max Malone Makes a Million,* Charlotte Herman

Introducing the Ten Basic Money Skills

This chart offers a guide to some of the activities and resources effective in this age range. You will see there are three to five activities listed for each skill. Experiment with these activities and ideas—they won't all fit your child, and you won't have time to do them all. Keep in mind that kids at this stage are very impressionable—great experience can make big impressions.

	Basic Money Skill	
	1. How to save	**2. How to keep track of money**
Actions: 5–8 Years	**Establish three containers for weekly allowance:** spending, saving, and giving. **Put a money message** under your child's pillow or in his school bag every other month (see sidebar on page 68 for suggestions). **Talk about the many ways we save things:** money, old clothes to give away, "the day," for a rainy day. What do these phrases mean and why do we use them? **Visit a bank** and open a savings account. Stop by frequently to deposit allowance or gift money and to make withdrawals. **Teach your child** how to spell the word *savings*.	**Have your child count the money he collects,** earns, or spends each week and write it down on a chart. Make this a regular task, connected to some other routine that helps it become automatic—and pleasurable (just before going on a walk with you, or just after a warm bath). Remember, you are trying to unhook the issue of money from anxiety whenever possible. **Select one thing** central to your child's life and have her be aware of the cost as a normal activity (dog food, soft drinks, or ice cream, whatever gets her attention on a regular basis). Carry this out for a year or two. **Ask your child to collect your spare change,** count it, and put it in coin rolls once a month. Take it to the bank and add it to her savings account. **Buy your child** her first wallet.
Resources	You can order kid-friendly "moneyboxes" for spending, saving, and sharing at www.moonjar.com *Sean's Red Bike,* Petronella Breinburg *The Money Tree Myth: A Parents' Guide to Helping Kids Unravel the Mysteries of Money,* Gail Vaz-Oxlade	*The Go-Around Dollar,* Barbara Adams *Dollars and Cents for Harriet: A Money Concept Book,* Betsy and Giulio Maestro *If You Made a Million,* David M. Schwartz *Eyewitness: Money,* Joe Cribb *The Berenstain Bears' Trouble with Money,* Stan Berenstain

An allowance is not a salary or an entitlement. It is a tool for teaching children how to manage money.

Big Tasks for Stage One

For this earliest stage of the financial apprenticeship there are six big tasks you can expect to accomplish:

1. Introduce your child to the Ten Basic Money Skills.

2. Start an allowance.

3. Observe and respond to your kids' money styles as they begin to emerge.

4. Communicate clearly to your spouse (and money mentoring team) your family vision and four or five big values you want to emphasize over the coming years.

5. Begin some savings programs for your kids. The power of compound interest is such that even very small regular deposits will have significant

6. Calm yourself; calm your kids. Money has such power to trigger emotional hot buttons that being conscious of what your money issues are and how they might affect your kids will benefit all involved.

By accomplishing these tasks, you will give your kids a sound introduction to the first stage of their apprenticeship.

1. Introducing the Ten Basic Money Skills

The Money Skills chart offers a guide to some of the activities and resources effective in this age range. You will see there are three to five activities listed for each skill. Experiment with these activities and ideas—they won't all fit your child, and you won't have time to do them all. Keep in mind that kids at this stage are very impressionable—great experiences can make impressions.

A n allowance is not an entitlement or a salary. It is a tool for teaching children how to manage money.

2. Starting the First Allowance: Trumping the Troublemaker

"But MaaaAAAAaaaa, it's my money; you can't tell me how to spend it."

"You can't make me clear the table for my allowance—I already made my bed, that's all I have to do."

"Come on... I need more money, my allowance isn't enough."

"Everyone gets more money then I do—and they aren't expected to pay for their own school lunch either..."

The allowance may be the most used and abused child training tool in America—and the biggest family troublemaker. It begins when kids are very young and parents dole out a few dollars a week in an earnest attempt to begin teaching financial responsibility. Unfortunately, too often the kids end up training their parents how that allowance will be used. Those little ones are so precocious!

We smile and chuckle over the child's attempts to be grown-up with her money. A quarter here, a dollar there, and soon her ability to hoodwink Mom, Dad, Grandpa, and Aunt Susie out of more money (because no one remembers what the allowance is really meant to cover) becomes apparent. And when that cute little tycoon morphs into a tyrant in the blink of an eye when frustrated by one of the allowance rules that pop up, it's tempting to give her another dollar to stop that whining.

Now, pay attention. Here is an important mantra, best learned when your child is at his or her youngest and cutest stage (and when you are most susceptible to clever manipulation by the little sweetie):

An allowance is not an entitlement or a salary. It is a tool for teaching children how to manage money.

Say it again, with conviction:

An allowance is not an entitlement or a salary. It is a tool for teaching children how to manage money.

If you decide to institute an allowance (and yes, it's a good idea), this is the message you must internalize and communicate to your children. Just like Tonka Toys are great tools for helping kids develop large motor skills, an early allowance can be used to help develop large money skills (saving, sharing, earning, counting). If it helps you remember, print this out in large type and stick it on your refrigerator:

Dear_____ ,

Your allowance is not an entitlement or a salary. It's a tool to help you learn how to manage money.

Love, Mom & Dad

The first allowance can begin with short, simple rules that are communicated often and clearly, such as:

- A weekly allowance is a way of helping you become an independent girl/boy.
- The more you learn and the better you handle money, the more quickly you will get additional responsibilities and privileges.
- There are six things to do with your money: Count it, earn it, save it, share it, grow it, spend it.
- Every three months, we'll take a look at how you are doing with these skills and see what changes have been earned.

Scenarios to Help Manage the Allowance

At the first hint that you are dealing with an emerging labor negotiator (with all due respect to those professionals!) or that an attitude of entitlement is creeping in, rescind part or all of the allowance and start over with your mantra: *An allowance is not an entitlement or a salary. It is a tool for teaching children how to manage money.* Keep this clear and you'll have fewer arguments about money in the household because everyone will know the rules. Here are a few scenarios to help you out:

Scenario 1: Six-year-old Natasha gets $6 per week from her mom and dad as her first allowance. "Can I spend this any way I want?" asks Natasha. The most effective answer is:

   a. "Of course, sweetie, it's your money."

   b. "No, you'll have to get our okay before you spend anything."

   c. "This is your learning money. This is money you will use to practice how to save and spend wisely."

The answer is C: This is your learning money. Remember, teaching kids to manage money developmentally is iterative. You will, over the years, repeat and repeat your themes. And though you may drive your kids crazy, they will learn and remember.

To make your message concrete (especially critical for the 5-to-8-year-old), place three jars, cans, boxes, or other containers on a shelf with your 5-year-old's name on the side of each: "Sam's Savings"; "Sam's Money to Spend"; "Sam's Money to Give to Causes."

Sam must count the money with you and then determine how much should go into each can. The amounts will vary with each family, reflecting financial values. Easy formulas are best when your children are very young: a third/a third/a third. The rules you establish must apply to all money that comes Sam's way, whether birthday money from Grandma, a few dollars for a chore you ask him to do, or some form of financial serendipity. Young children have not yet developed the sophistication to analyze money in complex ways. All they know is that it's cash and it came to them. If you do not have one rule that applies to all money when your kids are very young, you will be negotiating with über–financial analysts when they are 12.

Is this too harsh? Shouldn't children be able to enjoy the money that loving grandparents bestow? Can't birthday money be "exempt"? Of course you can devise your own rules—but be wary of communicating that money is handed out freely and can be used to buy stuff. Is that really what you want to tell your kid?

Scenario 2: Six-year-old Zoe has agreed to pick up her toys daily for a dollar-a-week increase in her allowance. This is:

a. A good way to introduce her to her first paid work.

b. An incentive to encourage her to be tidy.

c. A signal that being part of a family is a paid activity.

d. A bad idea.

The answer is D: A bad idea. Whether you have live-in staff to manage your household or struggle to make ends meet, the function of a family is to work, live, and love together. There are obligations and privileges that must be shared. Well-meaning parents who pay for beds made, dishes cleared, or toys and equipment stored properly give their kids conflicting signals about the nature of family—and are later puzzled when, as they get older, the same kids tend not to "pull together" as part of the family unit. Raise your daughter's allowance if she is handling her three money jars well and you have discussed how the extra dollar will be used. Pick some "special chores" that warrant extra-credit pay if you like. But don't tie an allowance to performing tasks that should be part of family life.

Scenario 3: Seven-year-old Matt has been faithfully putting all his money into his three money jars for two years. The cash in his "spending jar" as well as his "giving money away" jar has been growing because, as a hoarder, he didn't want to let go of any of the cash. You think it's great that he's turning into such a little saver. But by now the money adds up to several hundred dollars and you want him to open a bank account (a great chance to introduce the concept of compound interest and "making money while you sleep"). "No!" he screams. "I want it in my room!" You say:

a. "Okay, it's your money after all."

b. "An allowance is meant for you to learn how to manage your money. Hoarding it in cans shows me you aren't learning yet. We'll go to the bank in the morning and then start again."

c. "You won't get any more money until you agree to put what you have in the bank."

The answer is B. By telling your child he can do anything he wants with his money (hoarding, spending in silly ways, keeping it under his mattress), you abdicate your money mentor role.

And by threatening to withhold future money, you get yourself into an angry tug of wills. You are the grown-up. Keep this in mind and take the child to the bank—but don't go when one of you is cranky. Wait until you can go together in a sunny mood and combine the trip with a walk, some time spent in the park, or a bicycle ride.

Scenario 4: Aunt Meg has just come for a visit that happens to coincide with 6-year-old Anna's birthday. She gives her a really cute dress and a card that has $30 inside. With a gleam in her eye, little Anna says, "Thank you, Aunt Meg! Will you take me to the store now?" You say:

a. *"That sounds like fun. Let's all go together!"*

b. *"What a wonderful gift! Show Aunt Meg how you budget your money— she'll be so proud of you!"*

c. *"Now Anna, you know we agreed that all the money you get in gifts goes to your savings account."*

The answer is B. Encouraging kids to spend money as soon as they get it re- inforces the idea that holding on to it isn't important. But withholding a gift is a little hard-hearted. By encouraging her to treat the money as she always does, you reinforce the idea that all money must be managed for saving, spending, and giving away. Once part of the cash gift from Aunt Meg is in the spending jar, that amount can be used in a celebratory way, if Anna chooses.

Guidelines for Managing the Allowance

The following guidelines will help you manage your child's learning experience with an allowance. Relevant at each stage of the financial apprenticeship, they will help you navigate the tricky waters of kids and money:

Manage in the context of your goals. Are you trying to teach budgeting skills? Are you hoping to encourage independence? Allowances are less about financial transactions than about the learning opportunities that they afford. Decide what lessons you want to instill and then build the allowance plan around those lessons. Be clear about what you expect your child to learn and then hold her to those expectations.

Do not use the allowance as a tool for behavioral control. Money anxieties are deeply embedded in our psyches. Connecting an allowance to emotional or behavioral control exacerbates this and doesn't do much to help the child develop healthy financial habits. (I watch grown men and women cower at the very idea of dealing with their money because it triggers some deep, dark primal fear in their memory banks!) Using the allowance to reward or punish behavior distracts children from the main task of learning the Ten Basic Money Skills.

Remember that the allowance should be used as a tool, not an end in itself. Every year your child has an allowance, he should carry additional responsibility. If your 8-year-old gets $10 per week for trading cards and savings, when she's 9 she should get $12 per week and be expected to pay for whatever her collectible is, set aside savings, and set aside money for a charity. You may want to put your 15-year-old on a monthly budget if he has mastered the weekly responsibility of an allowance. But if 14-year-old Dylan hasn't learned to save money from his allowance yet, or 9-year-old Maya can't count change properly, don't increase financial privileges until the financial responsibility commensurate with that age/stage has been mastered.

Tailor financial categories to your children. Some families include a college savings category, others include a favorite sport or pursuit that may be expensive. If your daughter has horse fever, making her contribute to her passion will help her decide how serious she is. Categories also help reinforce values. If your family tithes to your religious affiliation, setting that goal early will send the message that that's an expectation. Starting a college fund for your child to contribute to, no matter how small, sends the message that college is a goal you hope he will pursue.

There is no right amount. I'm often asked "How much should we give our kids for an allowance?" Rule of thumb is to start small and increase the allowance as the child's ability to manage responsibility increases. If he is always borrowing against the next week, you may want to go backwards and help him manage smaller amounts—or take another look at the real budget and expectations of what the allowance is intended to cover. The point here is to learn how to manage money, not cultivate high finance. (Of course, there are special issues that come with the privilege of high-net-worth families. If your family struggles with "how much" when anything is really possible, see chapter 8.)

Remember that the allowance is yet another means to reinforce family financial values. The categories you stress, the expectations you are explicit about, the consistency of your attention to the allowance and its management will communicate your financial beliefs. Don't miss this center-stage opportunity to highlight your family's core money values.

3. Observing Money Styles

Remember the money styles referred to in chapter 1? How your child handles his allowance will give you information about his style, as well as how to mitigate its dark side. Let's revisit those styles in the context of your 5-to-8-year-old.

The hoarder. Because a child is under 10 is no reason to underestimate his intuitive ability. Often the hoarder has figured out that holding tightly to his money is a sure way to gain approval from mom and dad. Kids who figure out that saving equals parental approval will cover up a lot of other financial shenanigans with the chorus, "But gee, look how much I saved!" While saving is obviously one of the Ten Basic Money Skills we want to teach, hoarding is not. If the hoarder chooses to put 70 percent of his money into his savings jar and only 15 percent in each of his other money jars, that's fine—he's still learning the concept of *managing* money. To move things along, plan a special outing to spend the money on something of value or make a contribution to the Humane Society or a Children's Hospital. Be concrete and active and emphasize to your hoarder that the point of the money is to manage it, not just hoard it.

The spendthrift. Young children may be captivated by the magic of exchanging money for "stuff." Spending money for the first time may feel very powerful for a child who often feels "small"—and the adrenaline surge that some people experience when they spend money can be hard to resist. Helping your child feel powerful in other ways won't immediately curtail her urge to spend money, but making her conscious of her behavior is one way to manage it. The Ten Basic Money Skills activities are designed to help kids feel the sense of competency that is so crucial to their sense of well-being. The spendthrift is essentially a child out of control, and that inner sense of being out of control never feels good. Helping your child find ways to use her spending habits as a means of acquiring discipline and self-confidence is an important aspect of your work at this point.

Before your next trip to the mall, have your spendthrift make a list of things he wants to buy. Let him know how much money you will allow him to budget ($5 to $50), then give him Monopoly® money. Let him "shop," putting things in his basket, then help him add up what he's gathered. Compare this figure with how much "money" he holds. Has he stayed within the budget? If not, ask him to return the items he needs/wants the least. By putting him in control of money decisions, not just spending, you'll give him early practice in financial decision making—and increase his sense of personal power.

The scrimper. The scrimper may get real pleasure from coming home with change, and most parents will be wise not to tamper with such behavior. But if the scrimper also shows signs of withholding or selfish behavior with friends and family, it may be time to focus on the art of giving. As contributions to the "money to give away" jar accumulate, help your child select an activity or project to which she can dedicate the money. Set up a fund in her name at a local children's museum or build a relationship with a science museum where she enjoys going and can see her money at work. You can ask the museum's development director to meet with your child and thank her for her contribution; this will help make the connection more concrete and give her a sense of pride in having done something generous. In this way you can help your little scrimper see how money can be used for pleasure when put to work wisely.

The giver. Between the ages of 5 and 8, it is unlikely this behavior will show itself to any great extent—this is a highly egocentric stage of life and altruism is still nascent! But if you have a child who shows early signs of a constant need for approval, and who discerns that giving things away (toys, kisses, pictures) is a sure route to being liked, you may be getting early clues that you can watch as he grows older. We never want to discourage the generosity of a giving heart, but sometimes there can be a fine line between a genuine desire to give and approval-seeking behavior.

The beggar. "Can I? Can I?" is one of the most easily learned games in a child's repertoire. Usually it gets more pronounced over time as its success as a tactic for acquiring cash grows. Who has not given in to the game of "Can I?" just to make the sound go away? Next time, try one of these responses:

    a. I love you and I really like to make you happy, but "Can I?, Can I?" isn't a good way to get my attention. Why don't you go think about what you want and how else you might help me understand how important it is to you?

    b. No.

    c. Can you tell me how this fits into the budget we worked on last week?

All of these responses are fine—the important thing is to make sure you do not reinforce the "Can I?" game, which gets increasingly unattractive and self-defeating as the child grows older.

The hustler. To think of an innocent 5-to-8-year-old as a hustler is almost inconceivable. Yet the child who bargains for "just another ten minutes before I go to bed…" or who wheedles $20 out of his mom for a game his dad said he couldn't have or who tries to increase her allowance on a regular basis without real cause is developing early negotiating skills. While these skills are desirable in moderation, there is cause for alarm if the child shows a proclivity for getting away with something or regularly trying to get something for nothing.

Parents who are not straight with one another, either in money issues or other parts of their relationship, might explore what in their own behavior could be stimulating this tendency in their children. An effective tactic to counteract the hustler's schemes is to make sure that you, as parents, are in concert with one another regarding the decisions you make—then discuss those decisions with the child present.

The oblivious. A 5-to-8-year-old may already be aware that in the world of Mom and Dad, money equals responsibility. If it doesn't look like much fun, the child will quite reasonably "check out" when the subject of money arises. "There's only trouble here," may be the inner fear of the oblivious child. Your money mentoring team may be of particular benefit to this child. If Mom and Dad communicate anxiety about money, members of the team may be able to present a calmer, more engaging relationship with the development of money skills.

"I bought each of my five children everything up to a Rainbow Brite Jacuzzi and still I kept hearing 'Dad, can I get… Dad, can I go… Dad, can I buy…' Like all other children, my five have one great talent: they are gifted beggars. Not one of them ever ran into the room, looked up at me, and said, 'I'm really happy that you're my father, and as a tangible token of my appreciation here's a dollar.' If one of them had ever done this, I would have taken his temperature."
—Bill Cosby, *Fatherhood*

4. Family Money Values and Your Kids

Imagine that you're a guest of the sometimes irritating, often provocative, cranky talk-show host, Bill Maher, who asks a question about school prayer or military service. Whatever your views, your values probably would bubble to the surface in an instant. You know where you stand on these issues.

Now imagine yourself being interviewed by financial television journalist Brenda Buttner, who asks, "What key values do you and your family hold that determine how you handle money?" Chances are, the answer might not be on the tip of your tongue with the same immediacy as your position on military service or the death penalty.

It's likely there are words and phrases that come to mind: *save for a rainy day, be responsible, don't spend more than you earn, share with the less fortunate, practice frugality, take risks, be generous with your kids.* The list, as we shall see in a minute, may be long. But few families have conversations—as a unit—that make the values clear and operative. Often, the expectation is that handling money wisely is common sense or something that comes with age (if only!).

To pinpoint your family values, and whether you truly put your money where your mouth is, consider these questions for yourself:

- Do you feel deeply that we have an obligation to "give back"? Tally up the hours you volunteered last year, the pro bono work you did, or your total amount of contributions to charity. Do your actions match your beliefs?

- Do you subscribe to the notion that maintaining good health habits is basic to maintaining good health (and lowering health-care costs)? If you haven't worked out in months and your eating habits reflect a high-cholesterol banquet instead of a low-fat diet, you may need to reassess your values.

- Is *carpe diem* the family slogan? If your retirement fund is empty, you may be living out your principles. But if some part of you holds that saving for a rainy day is a value you care about, then you may be out of sync with yourself.

- Do you think of yourself as a committed environmentalist but you don't make a big deal of recycling with your kids?

- Do you believe that you and your kids must dress for success—even before you get there? You'll probably allot more to your clothing budget than your neighbors—and you may be more tolerant of your kids' clothing desires than if you believe a clothing budget needs to reflect the reality of your overall financial status.

Family Money Values		
	Mom	**Dad**
Earning	Earning lots of money isn't as important as being happy.	Being happy is earning a lot of money.
Spending		Everyone needs to contribute to the family "pot."
Investing	Safe T-Bills and a good savings bank is where I want to invest our money.	It's foolish not to take some risk to make money grow more quickly.
Saving	We should be saving as a family.	Only one parent's income should go to savings.
Philanthropy	Five percent of total income should go to a good cause.	Two percent of my income goes to my college alumni fund.

Financial values go well beyond the basics of "saving for the future," "sharing with others," and "spending wisely." Financial values are intimately tied to your most basic actions, to the way you spend your days and the feelings you have about how you relate to the world. How you live your life is central to what you will teach your kids about money.

Money Values at Odds

It's one thing to talk about family values and quite another to talk about the financial values held by individual members of the family. Pretending that everyone is on the same page with their values isn't enough.

Take a look at the chart below for an illustration of how the differing values of each member of the family can set the stage for sending mixed messages to your kids.

Daughter	Son	Aunt Em	Grandpa
Work? It interferes with my social life.	I want to work every weekend and after school.		
	It's my money —I can spend it any way I want.		Spend only on necessities. Luxuries are wasteful.
			Investing? I buy a lottery ticket every week, that's how I invest!
I can't afford to save now; I have expenses.		Enjoy life now; you won't live forever.	A wise man saves for the future.
	Why would anyone give money away?	My trust fund isn't large enough for me to give anything away.	Ten percent of my income goes to the church.

Some Values Descriptors

Power

Independence

Status

Peace

Generosity

Quest for knowledge

Desire for family

Community-building

Social justice

Love

Conservation

Family Money Values

It isn't likely that you'll be able to get all your family members on the same page in terms of values. But in the interest of being consistent money mentors with your kids, it does make sense to try to reach some kind of financial détente. Ivan Lansberg, author of *Succeeding Generations: Realizing the Dream of Families in Business*, describes the notion of a "Shared Dream" or vision that effectively helps galvanize family energy and excitement in the shepherding and growth of family wealth. Setting financial expectations is a lot easier when kids and parents are in accord in terms of a family vision: where will the family be in twenty years? What are the family's aspirations and hopes? Once the family vision has been articulated, the next step is to establish some clear values that your kids can use as financial lighthouses throughout their apprenticeship—and 5-to-8-year-olds are not too young to benefit.

To help clarify your values, you can make copies of the chart below. You and your spouse should first try filling it in separately. Share it with any other family members who are central to the financial life of the family. Use the list of words in the sidebar to help trigger your thinking about your values. Then discuss the results.

Family Money Values				
	Mom	Dad	Other	Other
Earning				
Spending				
Investing				
Saving				
Philanthropy				

Another approach to figuring out your financial family values is storytelling: think of a story from your life about each of the money issues in the chart below and analyze it to determine what values you hold about that aspect of money.

Now ask each member of your family to do the same. If your kids are young (under 12), turn this into an oral storytelling session. As you share your stories, both conflicting and shared visions about money will emerge.

The action	The story	The value embodied in the story
Earning		
Spending		
Saving and investing		
Philanthropy		

Getting values aligned among family members will go a long way toward ending family dramas related to money. Kids learn very early how to exploit parents' uncertainties and conflicting points of view. As a parent you have the authoritarian right to impose a decree: *we will have a set of values we live by as a family unit.* Here are a couple of tactics to help you build consensus on values:

Create a family chart, collage, or graffiti poster—any tool for helping family members articulate in some visual way the family vision and money values that are relevant to a *family unit* (as distinct from individual needs or desires). Little kids, especially, love making wall-sized murals. Put up giant sheets of paper with the words *saving, spending,* and *sharing* written in big letters. Ask your kids to draw an idea of what each word means. Then add the word *future* and have them do the same. The future is a pretty abstract concept for young ones. But having their moms or dads talk about the future is one way to give them a sense of what it actually means.

Don't try to take on too much. Try to locate one value at a time that will work for the whole family. For example: if giving back is an imperative that you hope your kids will adopt, make that a priority value to embody, model, reinforce, talk about, and act on. Or if taking time together as a family is a tradition you want to maintain, create a vacation savings pot and ask each family member to donate 1 percent of any money earned each month ($.03 if you make $2.50 stuffing envelopes for Mom this month; $50 if you make $5,000). The point here is to find common goals and vehicles for making your family's life values operational.

There is no one-size-fits-all path to clarifying your money values as a family. Every family has its own set of issues and needs. A single dad and his 6-year-old daughter will have different challenges than a two-parent family with five kids, two incomes, and a significant trust fund. But both families may share the same fundamental values—and that's the key: working hard to get your family money values in sync will go a long way toward helping you raise a family whose members are conscious and careful about how they spend, earn, save, invest, and give money away.

Principal x Rate x Time
$1,000 x 5 percent x 10 years = $500

5. Begin a Savings Program

Compound interest has been called the "eighth wonder of the world."

And no wonder—even a modest savings plan, growing over the course of twenty years can reap dramatic results. Visit www.bankrate.com to calculate a savings plan that will fit your own circumstances. Whether you have a sophisticated estate plan or are managing more limited resources, creating a nest egg for your child emphasizes the importance of savings, and can be a crucial part of helping him achieve independence.

6. Calm Yourself; Calm Your Kids

If money makes you uneasy, remember that lots of parents feel that way—but your job is to communicate to kids that managing money is as normal as brushing teeth. In this first stage, kids will approach issues of money through the eyes of influential grown-ups. If you're anxious and uncomfortable about money yourself, you will pass this attitude on to your kids.

Here are a few suggestions for finding the calm that will make your children's financial apprenticeship a much more pleasurable experience:

- Before taking your kids shopping, spend some quiet time with them— a warm bath, a short walk, even a few minutes of quiet talk and hugging can lower the excitement level considerably.

- Remember that when you're in a store, your kids are being intentionally and cleverly overstimulated. This is to the store's advantage and your disadvantage. Too much time spent looking, wanting, being revved up by the lights, the sounds, the visual displays will exacerbate your kids' hyperactivity. Limit the time and expectations of your kids while shopping. Decide what you are going to get before you go, and try to avoid turning the trip into a recreational afternoon.

- Help kids associate spending money with managing real needs, not filling empty places within the soul. Shopping to cheer up your kids, reward good behavior, or entertain them establishes patterns that will only be exaggerated as they grow older.

There are far more emotionally satisfying ways to cheer kids up (chicken soup and an hour spent playing a game together are quite effective), reward good behavior (gold stars and a note from you saying how proud you are), and entertain them (read to or with them, build something together, go for a walk together).

For some people, yoga offers another vehicle for calm in the context of dealing with money. In an interview for *Yoga Journal*, Linda Wolff, who owns and operates a boutique in New York City, said, "I see people in my shop doing this neurotic shopping, spending way more than they can afford. I recognize them easily. There's a certain look in their eyes, a nervous energy, sort of a rush or a high… I use to get that high myself, sometimes running up credit card bills of $30,000! I remember it used to feel great when I was buying. I'd feel free and alive—until I got the bill! It was like a disease. But my disease was cured by yoga. Something changed within. There came a calm, a balance, a feeling of being filled by myself and not by material stuff."

In another interview in the same magazine, Margaret Roche added, "Yoga helps me to maintain a peaceful attitude about money, as it does about all things. And it also helps me to budget. Because of yoga, I do not need to go out and spend money when I am feeling depressed. Instead I'll meditate, do some exercises, or paint."

You may not feel drawn to yoga as a way to calm yourself. But it's worth paying attention to any hyperactivity that emerges for you and your kids in relation to financial matters, and working to soothe counterproductive feelings.

Moving On

Stage One, "I'm just a kid," is a time to have fun with and enjoy the 5-to-8-year-olds in your life. They are curious, always exploring and discovering. When you can introduce them to something new that helps them master their growing world—while having a great time with you—you are launching great kids.

Money Messages

Think of these as financial fortune cookie–style messages.
Keep them simple and stick them in book bags, pockets, under pillows...

I love you more than all the money in the world.

Saving money is as important as brushing your teeth!

Being stingy is mean but giving money away too easily is silly! Love, Dad

A nickel as the same as how many pennies? A gold star for the right answer.

A dime is the same as how many nickels? A gold star for the right answer!

Find and save twenty nickels and I'll give you a crisp new dollar bill and a quarter! Love, Mom

Saving, sharing, and spending money wisely will keep you financially safe.

Only borrow what you know you can pay back.

Time is money. Use it well.

"Great is the human who has not lost his childlike heart."

MENCIUS (MENG-TSE), 400 BC

Stage Two
Ages 9–12: Encouraging Passions

Remember when you were 10 or 12 and suddenly everything seemed to matter deeply to you? It may have been when you first read *The Diary of Anne Frank* or *Black Beauty* or *To Kill a Mockingbird*. Or perhaps it was when you first saw *Old Yeller* or *High Noon*...

Those feelings, so tender and strong, help us as children move from a focus on self to a focus on others. We identify with characters in books and movies and cartoons and begin to have empathy for and interest in a world that is both reflective of and larger than ourselves. This is a time when best friends become all-important, when passions for hobbies or animals or causes first emerge. That awakening of awareness of the larger world brings with it a panoply of feelings, a sense that things really matter. This is the child who is now entering Stage Two of the financial apprenticeship.

Remembering these qualities as you choose money activities and resources from the following chart will help you make meaningful connections for the child who is morphing from a little kid to a "tween," perched on the edge of a new independence.

The Life/Money Map
Stage Two / Ages 9–12

Social / Emotional Development	Appropriate Money Skills to Master
Growing fast, body is changing	Can make change
Feels self-conscious	Shows initiating behavior and entrepreneurial spirit
Begins self-expression and independence	Shows awareness of cost of things
Developing social conscience	Shows awareness of earned money
Becoming aware of hobbies and careers	Can balance checkbook and keep up with savings account
Strongly identifies with peer groups	

Flip Open

3. How to get paid what you are worth	4. How to spend wisely	5. How to talk about money	6. How to live a budget
Help kids research the going rate for babysitting, lawn mowing, and other chores by interviewing friends.	**Organize a Mall Scavenger Hunt** (see page 34).	**Invite your child to write** a short play about loaning money to a friend who doesn't give it back on time. Offer to read the parts with her.	**Create a school-supplies budget with your child**, then take her with you to shop within that budget.
Role-play the part of a prospective client who asks, "What do you charge?" Let your child practice her response. (This is a good task to ask a money mentor team member to do.)	**Demonstrate how to read unit labels** on a product that matters to them (pet food, potato chips, juice)—is it cheaper to purchase an individual package, a multipack, or by the pound?	**Set a time to talk** about a family money vision.	**Give your child a budget for a weekend dinner** for the family. Let him create the menu and do the shopping for the dinner (accompany him or send him with one of his money mentors).
Send your child on a quest to www.monster.com. Ask her to find out how much a teacher, a lawyer, an astronaut, an actress, a bioengineer, a waitperson, and the director of a nonprofit make. Talk about why there are differences in salaries.	**Discuss the difference** between needs, wants, and wishes.	**In case of emergencies...** make sure kids know who to call, what to do, what their situation will be if anything bad happens to the family.	**Give your child a budget for something that matters to her:** books, CDs, or collectibles. Ask her for an estimate of how she'll spend the money, then have her account for it with receipts or with a notebook you can help her set up.
	Alert your child to the danger of accumulating interest on purchases. Charge interest on any small loans you make to him so he understands the concept in a concrete way.	**Ask your child** if she has any questions about money.	**Introduce the concept of utilities.** Show your kid your utilities bills and ask for ideas about how to lower them. Make sure you talk about how these fixed family costs affect some of the choices families make.
The Babysitter's Handbook: The Care and Keeping of Kids, Harriet Brown	A fun place for kids to learn about money and banking: www.kidsbank.com	BizWords, available through the online store at www.independentmeans.com	*Budgeting Know-How,* Marilyn Meltzer
The Ultimate Babysitter's Handbook: So You Wanna Make Tons of Money?, Debra Mostow Zakarin	A calculator to help your child reach a savings goal for a particular purchase: www.strongkids.com/tool/ladder.htm	*The Shelter of Each Other: Rebuilding Our Families,* Mary Pipher	*Kids and Money: Giving Them Savvy to Succeed Financially,* Jayne A. Pearl
Moneymakers: Good Cents for Girls, Ingrid Roper	*It's My Money: A Kid's Guide to the Green Stuff,* Ann Banks	*It Pays to Talk: How to Have the Essential Conversations with Your Family About Money and Investing,* Carrie Schwab-Pomerantz and Charles Schwab	www.escapefromknab.com
www.kidsmoney.org			

Parents need to talk with

their kids about money as comfortably

as they discuss the weather.

7. How to invest	8. How to exercise the entrepreneurial spirit	9. How to handle credit	10. How to use money to change the world
Order annual reports from your kid's favorite companies (Timberland, Netflix, Stonybrook Yogurt) and ask him to find out the name of the president of the company, how much money the company made in the previous year, and how much money it spent on marketing. **Ask your child to try to stump you with money words** taken from the financial section of the newspaper. Offer her a quarter for every word you get wrong. Or give her a list of words to look up, and a quarter for each one she memorizes. **Encourage your child** to choose something to collect that will gain value over time (stamps, fossils, comic books).	**Help your child** turn one of her passions into a small-business venture. **Read your child a story about an entrepreneur** who has turned a passion into a business. **Give your kid an Entrepreneur's Birthday Party.** Use the Product-in-a-Box Activity Kit for the main event. **Create an Entrepreneur's Hall of Fame.** Pay your child a quarter for each picture or story he collects about an entrepreneur he discovers. Make a gallery in his room for the pictures.	**Create a mock credit card** that can be used for purchases against your kid's allowance. **Offer to loan money for a special request,** and write a contract you and your child both have to sign. Charge interest if she exceeds her allotted time to pay you back.	**Have a family meeting** on a charity gift that matters to the whole family. **Ask your child to arrange a Goodwill or Salvation Army pick-up of family castaways** and have him estimate for tax purposes the value of the goods being donated. **Show your kid your tax return** and how you document the total amount you gave to charity last year. Explain what *tax-deductible* means.
An online broker for long-term investors: www.sharebuilder.com Information to help your kid become a successful investor: www.teenanalyst.com *Growing Money: A Complete Investing Guide for Kids*, Gail Karlitz www.lavamind.com	"Hot Company: The Money Game with Attitude": a board game that introduces entrepreneurship as a life option, available through www.independentmeans.com *African American Entrepreneurs,* Jim Haskins *The Toothpaste Millionaire,* Jean Merrill	*Credit-Card Carole,* Sheila Solomon Klass *Piggy Bank to Credit Card: Teach Your Child the Financial Facts of Life,* Linda Barbanel	Kids Care Clubs: www.kidscare.org Northwest Giving Project, involving kids in philanthropy: www.nwgiving.org/htm/inkids.htm *The Giving Family: Raising Our Children to Help Others,* Susan Crites Price (from Council on Foundations, www.cof.org)

The Ten Basic Money Skills

This chart will help you reinforce the big tasks of this period.

	Basic Money Skill	
	1. How to save	**2. How to keep track of money**
Actions: 9–12 Years	**Help your child set up a savings account** for a special interest, event, or goal. Make this an account that gets a regular deposit once a week or once a month that cannot be disturbed until the end of the year and is used expressly for the stated purpose of achieving a dream or goal. **Once a month, put a note under your child's pillow** or in her pocket with a message related to saving. An occasional email along these lines would work well, too! (See sidebar on page 92 for money message suggestions.) At this stage kids will have an easier time hearing you in a note than absorbing what may sound like a lecture. **Introduce other savings vehicles** like T-Bills, savings bonds, etc.	**If your child is getting an allowance, deposit it straight into a checking account,** and make sure there are one or two items in her budget that can be paid by check. Hold her accountable for a balanced checkbook before the next deposit. **Have your child write out checks for you** when you are paying bills, and/or let her tally the numbers as they are deducted from the balance. **Designate a regular activity** (movies with friends, purchase of a favorite comic book) for which your child will keep track of receipts for a month. **Make it concrete:** Ask your child to imagine a mile-high tower of dollar bills. It would contain over $14 million. **Institute a family currency** to teach the basics of how money works.
Resources	*New Moon Money: How to Get It, Spend It, and Save It,* New Moon Books Girls Editorial Board *Not for a Billion Gazillion Dollars,* Paula Danziger *The First National Bank of Dad: The Best Way to Teach Kids About Money,* David Owen www.orangekids.com	*Neale S. Godfrey's Ultimate Kids' Money Book,* Neale S. Godfrey *Hometown Money: How to Enrich Your Community with Local Currency,* Paul Glover www.madisonhours.org www.quicken.com www.kidsbank.com

The difference between

a fantasy and the realization of a dream

is having the financial skills

to make the fantasy come to life.

Big Tasks for Stage Two

There can be giant differences in maturation levels between a 9-year-old and a 12-year-old. The 9-year-old may still want to retreat to a tree house or her bedroom, or to the park with her friends, while the 12-year-old may long for more distant destinations and more elaborate activities. But their emerging passions and growing awareness are similar, so if you have children in this age range you'll want to attend to the following big tasks:

1. Offer Ten Basic Money Skills activities that will leverage your child's passions and her quest for independence at a higher level of challenge.

2. Help your child make independent money decisions in the face of fierce peer pressure. By establishing boundaries that will assist his ability to act on an established set of principles and values—in his life in general, as well as in his financial dealings—you provide both a guide and a "backup system" for his own emerging moral compass.

3. Make connections between developing passions and funding those passions. (The image of the starving artist or struggling writer may be romantic, but penury isn't a necessary ingredient in a creative life.)

4. Reinforce that the idea "behavior has consequences" must now be related to financial decision making. Making this connection helps kids develop a solid foundation for the next two phases of their financial apprenticeship.

5. Introduce role models. One of the ways you help young people experience a sense of reality about their passions is to give them access or exposure to people—including yourself!—who have pursued their passions into careers, achievements, avocations.

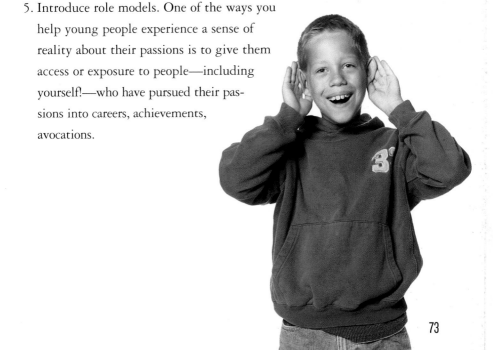

I. Ten Basic Money Skills: Encouraging Passions

The Life/Money Map for the 9-to-12-year-old assumes a greater level of self-reliance and self-expression than existed earlier, and takes into account the power of young passions. Those passions are a great vehicle for encouraging financial curiosity and responsibility within a context that matters to your child.

For example, if your 10-year-old declares she is a vegetarian, you can ask her to help you shop for food suitable to her life choice, giving her a budget that is comparable to what the rest of the family eats (and if you are all vegetarians, so much the better—food budgets are great teaching tools). Or if your 11-year-old son is well into collecting every NBA trading card, now is the time to explore the concept of saving and preserving—if you have a collection of your own to pull out or can demonstrate what the 1956 Mickey Mantle first edition is worth today, you'll be a real hit.

This stage is a good time to introduce the concept of entry-level jobs and salaries. In 2000, a survey done by Junior Achievement indicated that 24 percent of teens believed they would be millionaires by the time they were 30. Fueled by the get-rich-quick mentality of the Internet boom, many kids began to feel entitled to wealth at a precocious stage. Introducing your 9-to-12-year-old to the notion that entry-level NBA players are paid an average of $74,000 per year (still not bad) rather than astronomical Michael Jordan–sized salaries, or that a beginning doctor makes considerably less than an experienced surgeon—and that everyone pays taxes—helps establish more realistic expectations.

Many of the activities related to this stage are iterations of tasks you have done or resources you have shared with your children when they were younger. What's different this time around is *who they are*. Their growing ability to question and analyze will mean that their conversations with you will be more complex and interesting.

Milly and Lily are two 12-year-olds who just a couple of years ago were oblivious to the costs of the infrastructure of their lives. That they had a phone to use, transportation, food, and shelter was simply a fact of life, nothing to be considered a big deal. But on a field trip with a money mentor, the two girls were asked to create a "lifestyle budget." They made choices about what they wanted in their lives: the kind of car they could imagine driving, how much time they would spend talking on the phone, what their monthly clothes budget would be, how much they would eat, and where they wanted to live.

At 12 they now had context. Both girls went clothes shopping with their parents and understood the costs of fashion. Milly had a 15-minute-a-night phone budget. They understood that when their parents stopped for gas they had to pay for it.

As the girls made lifestyle choices, their mentor helped them tally up an estimated cost of each of their choices. Each girl made a set of choices that came to about $35,000 per year in costs. Then they fantasized about the kind of jobs they wanted. One had dreams of being a photographer and artist; the other wanted to be a teacher. They were selecting from life choices that seemed exciting and real.

But as they began to explore entry-level salaries for teachers in private schools (Milly's choice) and the time it takes to "make it big" as a photographer or artist (Lily's choice), both girls had a growing sense that they had to make the two visions—lifestyle and career—work in concert. At 12 they could now grasp that their dreams had a price tag that they had to plan for. This is the fertile ground of Stage Two. Kids needn't be discouraged by reality at this juncture, but they do need the right tools to deal with it.

This is also a time when you can help your kids dream Oprah-sized dreams—as she so eloquently puts it, "I dream so big it hurts my eyes"— and instill the notion that anything is possible. Too often, kids' dreams are pinched and small because grown-ups either pooh-pooh children's grandiose visions or treat them condescendingly. If children's dreams push up against the reality of what may be required to attain them, adults have a responsibility to guide them along their path with useful information and resources—not to squelch their passions altogether.

Skills for Passionate Lives

The difference between a fantasy and the realization of a dream is having the skills and financial acumen to make the fantasy come to life. By giving kids instruction in the language of money and business, as well as a vote of confidence that they are building the capacity to make their dreams come true, you are telling them "I take you seriously. I respect you and support your dreams."

Of course, it is also your job to instill responsibility and help your kids stay grounded. Parents who push kids to start businesses or reach for celebrity at a very early age may be working their own agendas and not those of their kids. But there is no harm in helping your kids think about what it takes to make a dream come true. The Ten Basic Money Skills activities will help you stick to reality while encouraging young passions.

Stage Two is often when family dramas kick in: tantrums about wants and wishes; anxieties about being different from or similar to peers; struggles around power and control. Sometimes these big tensions can seem unbearable to both kids and parents. But, at least where money is involved, kids who are clear about values and expectations will spend less time playing out big dramatic scenes than those who are trying to outfox you because the rules are not clear. And if you continue to create a calming environment in the financial spheres of your children's lives, you will mitigate those hormone-injected dramas.

2. Dealing with Peer Pressure and Money Decisions

This is the stage when, for kids, the stakes seem huge. To be in or out of the popular crowd matters. To be unique, but just like everyone else, is the impossible quest, and to be seen as "cool" seems imperative. It is at this point that parents become a critical counterbalance to the power of peers. Just because your daughter *says* everyone is buying Prada jackets doesn't make it essential for her to have one. And just because that new motorized bike is appearing in every driveway doesn't mean that you need to rush out and add one to all the toys already taking up room in your garage.

In spite of the rolled eyes and the world-weary "whatever," many kids would be perfectly happy to be out of the pre-adolescent rat race if their parents would just take them off the hook. If a kid can say to his friends "my dad is a jerk and won't allow [fill in the blank]," you get to be the bad guy and he can still seem cool. Parents who let their kids run the show, who abdicate their prerogative as the grown-up, give their kids no place to hide from their peers.

How to Handle Peer Pressure

The following real-life scenarios offer some ways to help your kids use money values to deal with peer pressure—and their own emerging passions.

Scenario 1: The sleepovers and play dates that 11-year-old Samantha and her friends had enjoyed since they were 5 or 6 began to evolve into weekly treks to the mall to see movies. Parents took turns dropping off and picking up the girls. Over time the movie date began to include an extra hour, then two, to hang out at the mall. But this also required extra money for food and the shopping that seemed an inevitable part of the mall experience.

Samantha's parents were increasingly uncomfortable with the amount of money she asked for every week, but they felt that it was important for Samantha to be part of her girl group and they didn't want to make her feel like an outsider. Though Samantha's affluent parents could well afford the outings, they were concerned their daughter was spending too much time "consuming" and not enough time developing herself in other ways. *What could they do?*

Scenario 2: Ray and Rex were 10-year-old twins who played for the same Little League team in their community. With five children to take care of, the twins' parents struggled to keep up with the purchases of equipment and uniforms for the boys, who seemed to grow faster even as spring turned into summer. The little boys loved the game and being part of a team was helping them develop individual personalities. The parents struggled with the tension of wanting to encourage their sons' team activities while juggling the family budget. *What could they do?*

Scenario 3: Twelve-year-old Ashley seemed mature beyond her years. Most of her girlfriends were a couple of years older than she. When Ashley began to press for money to buy clothes that looked more like those of her older friends and were inappropriate for her age, her parents faced the problem of how to rein in their daughter's sartorial tastes without making her give up her friends too. *What could they do?*

Scenario 4: Nine-year-old Roxie lived with her dad, a widower, and his new wife. Roxie's loving dad had been indulgent after Roxie's mother died, and the little girl had lived in a state of financial anarchy since she was 5. Whatever any of her friends did, Roxie of course wanted to do too—and Dad never said no. Roxie's stepmom was troubled by the habits she saw Roxie developing—spoiled and demanding—but both father and daughter resisted any attempts to alter the patterns they had developed between them. Dad was convinced that Roxie needed be "part of the club" and refused to set limits on anything she wanted to do with the "club." *What could the stepmom do?*

What would you do in these cases? How could clarity about family values and money have helped both kids and parents? When we put these cases to a panel of experienced parents, here are some of the suggestions they offered:

Scenario 1 Solution: The weekly movie is clearly as much a break for the parents as for the girls (having your tween occupied so you can get your own errands done is, after all, a great relief), so we don't want to disparage this activity too quickly. However, letting your kids turn into mall rats as a form of babysitting suggests a lack of imagination. A conversation among the parents of four or five girls could easily produce a schedule in which parents take turns once a month offering alternative activities to the mall. (This is a particularly good alternative for girls who find Girl Scouts no longer cool enough but who would still benefit from the structure and direction such organizations offer.) Cutting out the movie/mall trip altogether isn't necessary, but cutting it back from once a week to once a month can help make it a more special activity once again.

One parent might take the girls to a flea market or on a tour of garage sales and flea markets to hunt down quirky and inexpensive bargains—tracking down great vintage clothing or used CDs can be both fun and financially enlightening. Another parent might offer an afternoon of games or a video festival at home (popcorn and movie magazines for all). One parent could lead a hike or organize an afternoon volunteering at the local Humane Society, while yet another could provide cooking lessons, help the kids start their first investment club or charity circle, or get them started with a new hobby: collecting stamps, or creating photo journals to document their outings together. The idea is to give the kids ways to bond that do not rely on consumerism as recreation.

As kids get older and increasingly independent, parent-led activities get harder to organize. But with any luck, expanding kids' vision of how to spend their free time will have positive effects on the choices they make for themselves in the next stage of their apprenticeship.

Scenario 2 Solution: Parents whose incomes refuse to grow as fast as their kids are often hard-pressed to provide all the props required for many team sports, whether it's cheerleading or football, soccer or lacrosse. And having twins obviously doubles the dilemma. But once again, viewing other parents as a resource for all the kids can help your children cope with the pressures of a peer-driven world in which the purpose of a uniform is to appear uniform.

Working with the parents of all the kids on the team is one way to get a uniform and equipment "recycling" program in place. This has the dual effect of bringing down the cost of team participation for everyone while sending messages about sharing and conservation.

A recycling program that everyone uses also takes the stigma off the "poor kids." Children are highly sensitive about being seen as needy and may choose to drop out of sports rather than take part in a program that may require expenses beyond their parents' means. It will take some lobbying and organizing to have all parents participate, but a few phone calls to some of the parent leaders, and plans to set up the recycling center near the kids' playing grounds, will begin to make this resource the first stop—rather than a last resort—for all parents and kids.

Scenario 3 Solution: Ashley's dilemma is a common one for girls who are growing up fast and find themselves developing—both physically and social-ly—more quickly than some of their peers. Forcing girls to hang out with younger friends "just because" isn't very useful. Development has a life of its own—your best hope is to support it with some wisdom rather than to fight it.

On the other hand, there's no point in helping your daughter or son to move more quickly than is necessary—he or she may *look* and *feel* older and wiser, but do you really want your 12-year-old driving in cars with boys who are 16 and 17?

Ashley wants to express herself as a more mature young woman and thinks of clothes as a way to do that. Give her another option. This may be the time to revisit the allowance and discuss how handling one's money is a more enduring form of exhibiting maturity. Offer to increase her allowance to cover all clothing purchases. Suggest a trial period of three or six months to give her a chance to make a few mistakes and get on track again. (We all make buying mistakes—one bad choice is probably not enough to kill the experiment, but a pattern of belly-exhibiting shirt purchases but no socks may be enough to call the program off.) If, all along, the allowance has been treated as a teaching tool, not a salary or entitlement, Ashley will be able to demonstrate that she is gaining wisdom with her maturity. If not, the clothing allowance will be rescinded until she's ready for another try.

The key here is respecting your child's struggle to grow and mature, providing tools with which she can demonstrate to you and to herself—not to mention her friends—that she is in fact older and more "in charge." Indeed, if her older friends still can't balance a checkbook and are financially clueless, she may soon feel more grown-up than they! The more confident she feels about her money skills, the easier it will be to be her own person.

Scenario 4 Solution: In this case, the problem is less about peers and more about Roxie's father's reliance on her friends for signals about how to make her happy. Perhaps the best her stepmom can offer—like an aunt or close family friend—is another model of reality. While intervening in the established father-daughter dynamic may not be either feasible or effective, the stepmom can at least make sure she doesn't join the anarchy and exacerbate the problem. By keeping clear the expectations she has of Roxie when they are together, over time, both father and daughter may be able to let go of some of their old patterns. If not, that's a problem for the father to eventually deal with, or for Roxie to experience the consequences of—not the responsibility of the stepmom. But if the stepmom and father can establish a shared financial vision, it is likely that the entire new family will feel the benefits.

3. Making the Connection: The Cost of Passion

A child with a phenomenal voice can capitalize on that talent by working hard, studying with the best teachers, and devoting time and energy to the pursuit of his passion for music. Or he can hope he will overcome the odds, be selected for any of the myriad *Star Search* or *American Idol* TV competitions, and win the brass ring. If you don't have the good fortune to have the lottery-winning child in your household, a good backup plan is to encourage his passions in a reality-based fashion that nevertheless preserves the wild enthusiasm required to triumph over the typical challenges to dearly held visions.

Anyone who has ever raised a prodigy or even a moderately talented child knows that there is a financial commitment that attends such a pursuit. Frequently I hear parents talk proudly about children who are athletically, musically, or intellectually gifted in one form or another—then they follow the praise with a vow that they will "do everything possible" to help those children realize their potential. Rarely does that involve helping their kids be conscious and purposeful about how to meet the financial obligations of funding their heart's desires.

Thus we have young writers who believe there is virtue in poverty; spoiled children who strain or drain family resources while they feed their talent; and, worse, young people who hit the proverbial financial wall when they run out of funds for school or training or experiences that might well have provided the boost they needed to get to the top. Teaching kids to think about how to fund their passions will prepare them for the high-stakes pursuit of big dreams as they mature—and will embolden them to go after even bigger dreams. This requires a willingness to tell the truth and help kids confront real challenges. Here are stories of three families who have done just that.

Graciela, a young skater, was one of five children. She had been skating since she was 6 and at 11 had become interested in the competitive side of the sport. While it didn't seem she was on a track to the Olympics, Graciela was good enough to compete in regional and state events. This called for private coaching, skating costumes, long-distance driving to events, accommodation expenses, and myriad other details that accompany the world of kids and ice.

While financially comfortable, the family was concerned that funding Graciela's passion to skate competitively had the potential to draw resources from the dreams of their other children. Prepared to make sacrifices, they wanted to make sure the daughter was sufficiently committed to stay the course—and responsible enough to take part in the demands of the sport. They agreed to help her fund her dreams, but only on the condition that she be involved in the budgeting and decision making related to becoming a competitive skater.

The first year, Graciela's parents worked with her to draw up a list of all the annual costs of competing. They required two things of Graciela: that she make sure all expenses for her sport were recorded in a journal and documented with receipts, and that she take on an extra family chore to acknowledge the cost of her skating. She chose to be in charge of caring for the family's plants and weeding her mother's flower and vegetable gardens in the summer, and it was also her job to clean out and wipe down the family refrigerator once a month. None of the extra chores was inherently difficult, but as she carried them out she connected her desire to skate with the effort it took to make her desire possible.

Though Graciela won a number of competitions, by the time she was 18 she'd come to terms with the fact she was not of Olympic caliber. However, she was so committed to her avocation that she knew she would skate for pleasure for much of her life. And with each year she skated, she had taken on more and more of the financial responsibility for her activity, no doubt getting a head start on her decision to start her own company when she was 27. Handling money was second nature to her by then!

Twelve-year-old Rachel begged to have her parents pay for golf lessons. Her parents purchased a set of used golf clubs, took her to a public course to play a round of golf, and made arrangements for five lessons at the local parks and recreation department for $50.

Unfortunately, Rachel lost interest in the game after just one lesson; her fleeting interest took more time than she wanted from her other passionate activities. Her parents, rather than letting her simply stop the lessons, gave her a choice: see the commitment through or be prepared to use her babysitting money to pay them $40 for the unused lessons. Rachel was sufficiently uninterested in golf to forgo the rest of the lessons—possibly in the secret expectation that her parents would forget about the debt.

This was not the first time Rachel had reneged on a commitment to a new pursuit, so her parents decided to hold her accountable in this case. Rachel had an allowance of $20 per week; the money was to cover one movie or other weekly activity with friends, a beverage to go with the lunch she took to school every day, $5 for her savings account, and $2 for church. For eight weeks her parents subtracted $5 from her allowance and made it clear that she still had to keep up her church and savings contributions, leaving her short of money to go out with her friends. For two months she was forced to find ways of being with her friends that did not involve spending money.

It was a tough lesson, but Rachel's parents had watched a pattern evolve and decided that only a clear and strong message would break through their daughter's financial irresponsibility. The next time the question of funding a new enthusiasm arose, Rachel had a new seriousness about the commitment. She also learned to ask about cancellation fees and refunds—arrangements that provide the flexibility to change one's mind!

Ten-year-old Tyrone had been playing the piano since he was 4. He could read music with ease and was composing by the time he was 7. Tyrone's parents lived in a school district that offered very good music instruction, and his teacher had, for a modest fee, agreed to give him private lessons on weekends.

When the local school district, in a round of cost cutting, eliminated the school music program, Tyrone's parents were devastated. They were unable to afford additional private lessons of the caliber he was used to and could not see how they were going to support his gift. At their wits' end, Tyrone's parents did respect their son enough to discuss the terrible dilemma with him. Heartbroken, they announced that he would have to take some time off from his lessons until they could save money to hire a new tutor or could find another public school with an advanced music program.

But Tyrone was a step ahead of them. The precocious boy mentioned that he had met a few people who had come to hear him play at the school, and perhaps one of them would give him lessons if he had something to barter. The parents were not enthusiastic about putting a 10-year-old out to earn music lessons, but the idea did trigger them to explore options in the community. Eventually they struck a deal with the music director of a community church. In exchange for Mom working four hours a week in the church soup kitchen, Tyrone could have lessons with the church music director.

Eventually the family did get their son enrolled in another public school with a good music program, and the young boy continued his studies. This is not a fairy tale in which the young prodigy finds a fairy godmother who sends him off to Juilliard and he goes on to win the Van Cliburn competition. It's a story of a family who, rather than hide a difficult reality from their child, engaged him and gave him a chance to be part of the solution.

Children who feel helpless and hopeless because information is withheld from them will grow up with the long-term consequences of being left out of problem-solving opportunities. It is sometimes lack of information that makes kids turn away from financial responsibility—if something seems mysterious and outside their ken, they may sense danger and put the blinders on. If you want your kids to be responsible for pursuing their own passions, you have to include them in real-life discussions and decisions.

Stretching Visions

Making the connection between financial responsibility and the pursuit of passion is part of the work of Stage Two; helping your child expand his vision of what is possible is another part. These are the years when the first entrepreneurial urges may show up. The budding desire to have a business may present itself as a form of play, but parents would do well to take such ideas seriously and encourage some basic enterprise. This is a new interest, a curiosity at work. Channel it.

If your 10-year-old wants to set up a lemonade stand (or a more contemporary venture—say, fresh-squeezed orange juice or healthy muffins), go along with the activity, but make sure she adds up the cost of the ingredients to determine how much to charge for each item. And if she wants to set up shop outside the house on a street with no traffic, help her find an alternative location where she will actually get some business (maybe an aunt or a good friend lives on a busier street).

Always connect your kid's enterprise to something bigger than herself: What will she do with the profits? How will this idea make the community a better place? How might the business make a difference to friends and family? Can your child imagine being responsible for more than one lemonade stand around town?

Condescending to children ("isn't that cute, honey" or "you have no idea what you're doing" or "don't be silly") is a lost opportunity to take advantage of a "teachable moment." You don't want to badger your kid with an obsessive attention to money at every turn, but you do want to acknowledge that your "little girl" or "little boy" is beginning to think, act, choose, and see herself or himself in new ways. Supporting that growth will give your child a leg up in the next stage of development.

A question I sometimes get from families of high net worth is, "My child really doesn't have to work. He is set for life. Why should I encourage money-making activities if they aren't necessary?" I answer with questions of my own: What kind of child do you want to raise? What kind of higher purpose do you hope your child will aspire to and how will you prepare him to achieve it? In chapter 8 we will explore in depth the special issues of high-net-worth kids. For now it is enough to say that children at all income levels who master experiences that offer reward for work tend to have greater self-confidence and self-worth than those whose primary activity has been to consume or to satisfy themselves. Even kids who have the opportunity to delve deeply into studies or pursuits that may not be financially fruitful (life as a painter or poet, for example) find that they feel better about themselves if they know they possess the savvy to be financially independent.

Connecting work with earning money is valuable in developing responsible work habits, acquiring discipline, and understanding the need to make hard choices. Who doesn't have an image of the Girl Scout who sells more cookies than anyone, or the newspaper delivery kid who shows up reliably every morning? These children are developing work habits that tangibly demonstrate

---

Connecting work with earning money is valuable in developing responsible work habits, acquiring discipline, and understanding the need to make hard choices.

---

the connection between labor and reward; drive and fulfilling passions. From working with kids at Independent Means, it has become clear to me that those who start early have an easier time mastering those skills than the kids who aren't required to work for pay until after high school or even college.

So how can your Stage Two kids earn money? Here are suggestions that some families have shared with me:

Make your kids "subcontractors" for your work projects. Is there something you can delegate? Stuffing envelopes? Paying by the number of envelopes stuffed gives a tangible sense of value. Entering addresses into your Palm Pilot? Fifteen cents for every address will do it for the 10-year-old; the 12-year-old may demand a little more. (Some kids will handle this task more quickly and easily than you can.)

> **Good Moneymaking Chores for Kids**
>
> Polishing dad's shoes
>
> Washing mom's car
>
> Watering plants for a neighbor
>
> Reshelving books
>
> Walking the neighbor's dog
>
> Organizing dad's tool closet
>
> Addressing party invitations

Hire your kids for special personal projects. Cleaning up their rooms should be a normal part of their own responsibility; however, refolding all of your sweaters and putting them away, cleaning up those drawers into which you throw odds and ends, polishing your shoes, or reshelving the books or CDs you have left out deserves compensation. Other extras might include helping to plant seedlings in the spring, putting away lawn furniture in the fall, or helping a relative or friend with chores.

You might keep a running list of possible "projects for cash" posted in the kitchen. Whenever your kids plead boredom, have them select a project and earn some money for their saving, spending, and giving jars.

The respect that comes from work performed outside the home is often very satisfying for kids. Walking the dog or feeding the fish and guinea pigs at home is part of family duties; walking or washing the neighbor's pets is an opportunity to earn extra income. Help your kids create flyers to post in the neighborhood for whatever service they're interested in offering.

As your kids' entrepreneurial instincts kick in, help them turn ideas into money. Is the garage or attic in need of a serious cleaning out? Offer to share the proceeds of a garage sale with your kids if they help out. Make sure the help is real (marking prices on items for sale, helping to select what will be sold, setting up tables, making posters and flyers to advertise, being present at the sale to help with customers and make change). At the conclusion of the sale, make sure you calculate the profits with them by deducting any costs that are appropriate.

If your child wants to start her own business, help her devise a business plan. Whether it's a proposal to run birthday parties for younger kids or to sell those fishing flies she makes, helping her walk through the basics of who her market is, what the cost of the product or service is, what she will charge, and how she will market her goods will get her thinking about the kinds of questions and puzzles she needs to solve to make money.

One of my favorite stories is of 11-year-old Corey. He saw a moneymaking opportunity in the fact that the local softball teams playing in a field near his house drew a crowd every weekend, but there was no hot dog stand or anyone selling soft drinks to the spectators. Corey talked his mother into taking him to a discount store where he bought several cases of soft drinks. The next weekend he bought ice, piled it into a red wagon left over from his "childhood," then hauled the wagon to the game. He sold out in an hour. Corey quickly became a fixture at the games, providing a much-needed service.

As he grew more confident, he decided that he wanted to branch out. Because it was summer, he had all the weekdays off in between the games, so he decided to take his wagon closer to town and try to sell soda to the tourists who came to visit during the summer. Again, his business did well: out-of-towners were charmed to buy from a boy selling soda out of his red wagon, and as he was a sociable child, they also learned a little about the town.

Corey's business was going great guns until one of the local merchants (a true Scrooge of a character) turned the boy in to City Hall for operating a business without a license. Suddenly the 11-year-old was thrust into battle with the bureaucracy. But his mom was a great advocate for her son. Together the two of them learned what was required to get a business license, and by the time school started, Corey was the youngest person in California to have a business license. Imagine learning at 11 what it takes some people another twenty years to do!

> **Suggested Nominees for the Entrepreneur's Gallery**
>
> Tom and Kate Chappell (of Tom's of Maine toothpaste)
>
> Ben Cohen and Jerry Greenfield
>
> Oprah Winfrey
>
> Monica Lozano, President and CEO of La Opinión
>
> Roxanne Quimby, Burt's Bees cofounder
>
> Tiger Woods

Another means to stretch the visions of the 9-to-12-year-old is the Product-in-a-Box Activity Kit (available from www.independentmeans.com), which is great for birthday parties or rainy weekends. This "First Business Plan" activity gives kids a chance to create and invent a product or service and draw up a business plan for it. Effective with multiple groups of four to six kids, Product-in-a-Box gives kids a chance to exercise their considerable imaginations while transforming ideas into earning exercises.

4. Behavior Has Financial Consequences

The 9-to-12 years are prime time for helping kids learn to make choices—sometimes hard choices—that will have long-term consequences. This is not an age when delayed gratification is very appealing and you may end up having to endure tantrums and the nag factor, but keep in mind that you're the grown-up and that's part of your job.

Some families use themselves as "case studies" to help their kids connect the dots between choices and money. When his children were young, W. Bruce Cameron, creator of the very funny column on which the sitcom *8 Simple Rules for Dating My Teenage Daughter* is based, wrote a piece for *Time* magazine describing a radical approach to financial awareness. He reported that to get his kids' attention he printed out a Quicken account of the family finances, showing every penny of income and "out go" for the family, sparing no detail. (He did take some time to explain to his children the nature of the trust he was bestowing on them with this information—and his expectation that they would not betray that trust by blabbing the information to their friends.) He described the experience this way:

At first my children were shocked to see how much money I made—wow, we were rich! But then I showed them how much money the government took off the top, how much we spent, and how little was left at the end of the month. When they saw our credit-card balances, they actually got angry: Why hadn't I done something about this earlier?

The results of the family meeting were immediate. My children had always rolled their eyes when I suggested that not every single light bulb had to be turned on in an empty room; now they could clearly see the toll that utilities were taking on our budget.

My kids now consider putting on a sweater a viable alternative to goosing the thermostat. They understand when we pass up pricey treats at the grocery store that it is not because their parents are determined "never to have anything good to eat" as they have charged, but because we need to feed a whole family for an entire month.

Cameron's solution will not be for everyone, but since reading his account I have heard many parents describe similarly positive results with this approach. Families that are uncomfortable talking about money may find this a hard strategy to implement, but my experience is that when given real information, kids, like anyone else, will rise to the occasion and use it wisely.

Obviously, if there is a good deal of money "left over" the issues are a little different. But the principles are constant. Helping kids understand early on the connections between the options they have and the choices they make is one of the most important parental tasks you can accomplish. I meet too many adults who describe with a measure of real sorrow how hard it is to say no to the things they want and how they cannot escape their chronic state of debt.

To give your kids practice making choices, use the activities listed in the Life/Money Map above or try these additional exercises:

- When your kid asks for brand-name shoes or a new high-tech toy, give him this choice: you can have X or you can get something similar but less costly and keep the amount left over to put into your savings account.

- If your daughter asks to go to a movie, offer to put the money she would have spent into her savings account and rent a movie to watch with her instead.

- If your son's birthday is approaching, offer him a choice of getting a present from you or selecting a stock he can follow that may appreciate (or decline) in value. (Younger kids may turn this one down, but asking the question has some intrinsic value.) Make the stakes bigger over time. Give your kid the choice of going to a summer camp in another state or attending one nearer your home and donating the money you'll save on travel to a cause she cares about (Surfrider Foundation, Girl Scouts, Humane Society).

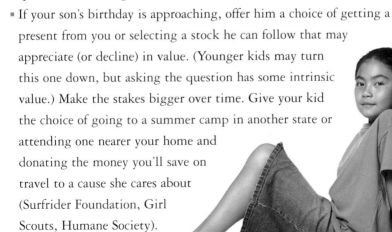

- Is your kid spending more on CDs and DVDs than you're comfortable with? Let him know that he'll need to make up the difference somewhere and ask which he's willing to give up: eating out or movies with friends for a month? Another option is to ask him to select a paying project around the house to help compensate for the extra money he's spending.

In 1985, children aged 4 to 12 influenced about $50 billion of their parents' purchases each year. By 2000 that figure had quadrupled to over $200 billion. Kids are targets because companies are well aware that a nagging child can wear down a parent's resolve not to buy something more effectively than an ad campaign targeting the parents. This parental capitulation not only fills the coffers of companies but also undermines your children's ability to connect their choices with real financial consequences.

5. Introducing Role Models

Parents who share their own passions with kids offer a living role model, demonstrating that life is full of zest and wonder and that being financially responsible is part of what makes it so. Making it clear that you set aside part of your budget to support an environmental cause, help keep the local health clinic open, or fund a choral group you care about (or perform in) is a way of helping your kids see you as a whole person, more than just Mom or Dad.

Being open about the activities and issues that move you, and talking about them to your kids, is also a form of money talk. Whether sharing the challenges of raising money or exulting over the triumph of meeting a fund-raising goal for one of your pet projects, this conversation will become a normal part of what kids associate with achieving something that matters deeply to them. Whether adding to their vocabulary words like *balance sheet*, *capital*, and *budget*, or talking about the normal frustrations and joys of matching financial wherewithal with talent and vision, parents need to talk money as comfortably as they discuss the weather.

It's a good idea to make sure your kids meet—and spend time with—the people you know who have combined their passion with their vocation. If you are having friends for dinner who fit this bill, set aside a little time for the kids to spend with them. You don't need to interrupt all your grown-up time, but exposing kids to people who can offer multiple visions of a passionate future will expand their horizons.

Moving On

In this chapter I've discussed how to make financial issues relevant to kids in the context of their growing enthusiasms. While their attention spans may still be short and they will lurch sometimes from powerful interest to new passion in the course of a week, it's important to remember they are just experimenting with their new world—trying it on for size. In this stage of the financial apprenticeship, the Ten Basic Money Skills can function as place markers on the journey.

In the next chapter I'll address the changing needs and attitudes of the teen who is experiencing a growing imperative to seek independence.

Money Messages

Messages to send in emails, hide under pillows, or stick into book bags...

I care about your dreams. Saving money is one way to make them come true. Love, Mom

As you develop your sense of style, let's talk about ways to look great and spend wisely too. Love, Dad

Sometimes saying no to friends is a special form of courage.

I love your idea for making hats for your friends. Go for it!

Wise men save for the future. Foolish men spend what they get. Proverbs 21:20

Imagine that you have $10,000 to give away to a cause you care about. Tell me what it would be and why.

Is there an idea you have that you would like to turn into a business? Tell me about it.

Can you suggest five things your dad and I can do to save money for a family vacation?

Going to school is an investment in yourself.

A social entrepreneur uses her imagination and resourcefulness to help solve problems in the community. How can you be a social entrepreneur?

I like the way you are managing your allowance—it makes me proud.

Money acts like gas in a car—it helps fuel your passions. Tell us what your passions are so we can plan how to save money to fuel yours.

" Let him step
to the music which he
hears, however
measured or far away. "

HENRY DAVID THOREAU

Stage Three
Ages 13–15: Breaking Away

Stage Three is both exciting and challenging. The tensions inherent in becoming a true individual with ideas and values that may begin to diverge from Mom's and Dad's make themselves felt during these years. On the one hand, your kids are developing more complex and interesting personalities; on the other hand, complexity is not easy. Just at the time you feel that your children should become more fully responsible for their financial actions, they are trying to assert their own individuality at every turn—often by making it clear that what you want is no longer as important as *who they are becoming*.

But don't let their natural attempts at self-expression deter you from the goal: *raising financially fit kids*. Achieving this goal in the context of a turbulent developmental stage isn't easy, but this stage will pass; your children's need for a solid financial foundation will endure.

The Life/Money Map
Stage Three/Ages 13–15

Social / Emotional Development	Appropriate Money Skills to Master
Focuses primarily on the present; has only a vague sense of the future	Can shop comparatively
	Understands relationship of time to money
Egocentric, self-conscious, and anxious about personal behavior	Begins to earn money; initiates small ventures
Begins to think independently	Commits to saving goals
Conforms to peer group norms and behaviors	Develops basic understanding of investment
Highly experimental phase; tries on different roles	Connects money and future
	Understands philanthropy
	Can read bank statement
	Understands interest and dividends

Flip Open

3. How to get paid what you are worth	4. How to spend wisely	5. How to talk about money	6. How to live a budget
Check with your money mentoring team to see what work for pay they may be able to offer your teen. Let them know you want to have your child research and negotiate for the pay. **Send an email to your teen** that says "Salary comes from Latin word *salarium*, meaning 'salt allowance.' Roman soldiers were given a salarium as part or all of their income." Remind your child that she is blessed not to be a Roman soldier! **Give your kid a list of ten jobs** and ask him to search for the average pay of each on the Internet (see sidebar on page 101 for job suggestions). Ask him to find entry-level salaries and salaries for ten years' experience.	**Introduce the idea** of a warranty or "insurance policy" next time you fill one out for one of your purchases. **Give your kid** a subscription to *Consumer Reports* magazine for Labor Day. **Explain** what a hidden cost is. **Have your child find** competitive prices for lessons or purchases. **Explain what an impulse buy is** and why candy bars are placed near cash registers.	**Talk about ads** shown on your kids' favorite TV shows. Ask them to critique for qualities such as accuracy, honesty, and value. **Discuss the difference** between accumulation (saving) and consumption (spending). Talk about the environmental and human implications of each.	**Start a special-category budget** for one of your child's favorite activities. **Have your teen plan and budget** for a family outing. Put him in charge of everything required for a full day, including gas, food, tips, and entry fees. Give him cash at the stat of the day to pay for each part of the event. If he runs out before the day is over, don't bail him out; go home early and try the exercise again in a month. **Use the Fourth of July (Independence Day)** as the annual review date for allowance increases. Make sure the symbolism is not lost on your son or daughter.
Job-finder website with lots of info and resources: www.monster.com Another great job-finding site: www.careerbuilder.com A complete online course on baby-sitting: www.baby sittingclass.com	Subscribe to "A Real Life" newsletter, (802) 893-7040 *The Millionaire Next Door: The Surprising Secrets of America's Wealthy,* Thomas J. Stanley and William D. Danko *Consumer Reports* website: www.consumerreports.org	*What You Owe Me,* Bebe Moore Campbell *Green Talk: Money: How to Get It… Keep It…Avoid Getting Ripped Off!,* William R. Hegeman	A website exploring the purpose, potential, and challenges of financial wealth: www.morethanmoney.org Money Camps are a fun place for adults, kids, and families to learn about money management: www.moneycamps.com An education program that stimulates learning about economics and finance: www.smg2000.org

Financial candor, like an

expectation of good manners, should

be part of daily family life.

7. How to invest	8. How to exercise the entrepreneurial spirit	9. How to handle credit	10. How to use money to change the world
When you come across articles about the companies behind your teen's favorite brands, ask her to read them and tell you whether she feels the companies sound like risks or solid investment possibilities. **Introduce the idea of socially responsible investing.** Ask your child to research and track three companies (preferably those making products he uses) and let you know which is the most socially responsible and why he thinks so (see below for research resources). **Buy stock** in a company that has meaning to your teen, review the annual report with him, and visit the company's website for interim news.	**Give your teen** a biography of an entrepreneur. **Suggest that your child and his friends** run a neighborhood car wash to raise money to buy holiday gifts. **Send your kid an email** with information about a business plan competition she can enter.	**Give your child your credit card bills** and ask her to tell you how much you are spending each month on interest. **Ask your child to go online** and see if he can find a credit card that would charge lower interest than your current card. Make the switch if he finds a better deal. **Explain** what a credit report is.	**On Valentine's Day give your teen $50** to make a contribution to a cause that's "close to her heart." **During the next state or national election, ask your child to read about and select a candidate** he wants to give money to. Offer to match his contribution to that candidate's campaign. **Make a contribution** to Emily's List in your daughter's name.
When I Grow Up I'm Going to Be a Millionaire: A Children's Guide to Mutual Funds, Ted Lea and Lora Lea A publication for environmentally friendly investing and business: www.greenmoney journal.com www.tipsforkids.com	"Hot Company: The Money Game with Attitude," available through the online store at www. independentmeans.com *Girl Boss: Running the Show Like the Big Chicks*, Stacey Kravetz *African American Entrepreneurs*, Jim Haskins	*Credit Card Nation: The Consequences of America's Addiction to Credit*, Robert D. Manning An educational "mini-lesson" on credit cards: www.NICE.emich.edu/ teens.html www.qspace.com	Nonprofit organization devoted to encouraging kids to work together to improve their schools and communities: www.whatkidscando.org *Volunteer Vacations: Short-Term Adventures That Will Benefit You and Others*, Bill McMillon, Doug Cutchins, and Ann Geissinger www.thewishlist.org

The Ten Basic Money Skills

This time around, the Ten Basic Money Skills activities will be used to support and reinforce the connections between independence and reponsibility, giving kids tools to shape themselves into people with depth and substance.

	Basic Money Skill	
	1. How to save	**2. How to keep track of money**
Actions: 13–15 Years	**Find a goal connected to independence** and set an expectation for your child's contribution to that goal. Whether looking ahead to owning a car in a couple of years or going on a class trip, some of the money for this undertaking can come from a dedicated savings plan. It may be small, but it must send a message: financial planning equals independence. **Write a letter (or an email) to your child.** Discuss your own experience with learning (or not learning) to save and the effect it has had on your life and independence. Ask three people your child knows and respects to do the same. **Revisit the effect of compound interest** on the money your child saves. Perform a calculation that relates to her savings habits.	**If you haven't already, now's the time to start a real checking account.** Take your child to the bank and open an account. Give his allowance to him by check to cash or deposit, and plan regular trips to the bank so he can perform the transactions himself. **Follow that dollar:** ask your kid to keep a diary of every penny spent and earned for one day. Review the day's expenses with him. Now have him keep a diary for three days. Extend to a week and then a month. Ask your child to make observations about his own money styles and habits. What does he want to change or improve that might have an impact on his desire for independence? **Ask your child to follow you** one Saturday and keep track of every penny you spend. What advice does he have for you?
Resources	*20 $ecrets to Money and Independence: The DollarDiva's Guide to Life,* Joline Godfrey *Countdown to a Thousand Dollars,* Lisa Kerber Resources about saving wisely and getting the best return on your money: www.teenadvice.about.com www.yacenter.org	A fun approach for kids to learn financial strategies: www.escapefromknab.com *Money Matters for Teens,* Larry Burkett Classroom edition of the *Wall Street Journal*: www.wsjclassroomedition.com/teen/index.html

Financial literacy is not
just about the money, but about
launching great kids.

Big Tasks for Stage Three

The big tasks in this stage include the following:

1. The Ten Basic Money Skills are revisited in a yet more sophisticated fashion. Kids can and should be held accountable for their financial behavior.

2. Helping your teen make a conscious connection between financial responsibility and personal independence (including making a budget more than just an intellectual exercise) will give her or him a growing sense of maturity.

3. As present-oriented as kids are at this stage, now is the time to help them begin to stretch their vision into the future.

4. Though the teen years are still a time of self-absorption, providing experiences and opportunities to think outside the self is increasingly important.

5. With all the effort you may make in raising a financially fit child, you may still encounter the "dark side" of financial literacy. Your task is to tune in to any warning signs that your child is not developing sound financial skills, and intervene as necessary.

1. The Ten Basic Money Skills, Round Three

This time around, the Ten Basic Money Skills activities will be used to support and reinforce the connections between independence and responsibility, giving kids tools to shape themselves into people with depth and substance.

2. Making Connections between Financial Responsibility and Personal Independence

Not too long ago I met with officers of the Salvation Army, exploring ways to integrate financial literacy skills into programs they offer in the community. The captain I spoke with said to me, "We are concerned about the spiritual well-being of the people who come to us, but if we do not also help them develop skills to stand on their own, we are letting them down. Providing financial literacy," he remarked, "is akin to the concept of giving people the skill to fish rather than handing them fish to eat." The goal of this leader in the Salvation Army was to find a way to start teaching people how to make the connections between learning basic financial skills and taking care of themselves.

Across the economic spectrum, the desire to help kids develop into well-rounded people who contribute to family and community is universal. And while many parents would love their kids to live on Easy Street, the fact is that families that rob kids of the opportunity to develop skills of independence do them a great disservice—not just in the short term, but in the long run as well.

Moving the Conversation to a Higher Plane

By now your kids know that money equals independence. The mantra for allowances we set forth earlier (see page 54) is now joined by a corollary: *the more financially responsible you are, the more independence you will earn.* (You can give your kid a T-shirt with this motto printed on the back if you think it will help!)

These are the years when teens want to start dating, go more places with friends without parental supervision, travel, stay home alone, make decisions for themselves, and experiment with new tastes and experiences. Too often, conversations about these opportunities and adventures turn into fractious tugs-of-war that have more to do with authority and control than with the issues of independence they are really about.

Writing for the journal *More than Money*, Ann Slepian demonstrated how to move the discourse with your kids to a higer level:

When I say "no" to something my son wants to buy or do, I have coached him to ask me, "what will help?" I then think out loud: "Well, on the one hand, I want you to learn how to budget your money and save for the things you really want. That's a really important skill in life, one that many adults don't know well enough. That's one reason I ask you to rethink the need to spend money on this (trip, item, etc.). On the other hand, it's something that may help you grow as a person and I'd be willing to pay half the cost if you really want it. But I will want you to pay me back if you don't use the money well and wisely."

Sometimes, by thinking out loud I find creative ways to address whatever concerns I really have about the request that led me to say no initially. Other times it seems nothing will help. The answer is still no. He's still mad at me, but he can see I'm not just being an arbitrary authority.

Shifting the level of discourse from a war of wills to a collaboration in search of a solution is one way to help your teens begin to see the power of problem solving. It is also the most effective way to help them develop good judgment in service of their own independence. Along the lines of "what would help?" you might try these approaches:

How will this trip, action, choice affect your budget, savings account, plans for the future, checking account? Getting your child to make the connection between choices and financial impact is a habit best learned when she has something at stake. For example, suppose you have already created a financial plan for the year when a new opportunity crops up. Whether or not you can easily afford to fund the unexpected event is less important than that your teenager examines the opportunity in light of the plan already in place: is there something he can give up later in the year? Is there a way to earn some extra money to make sure the budget is still balanced at the end of the year? He will be facing this challenge of resources throughout his life, whether he becomes a teacher in an inner-city school, the head of a nonprofit, the head of a household, or the CEO of an Inc. 500 company.

How can you show me that you have the sound judgment and discipline to make this a good financial decision as well as a fun choice for you? Going on a backpacking trip in one of the national parks with one's friends, without an adult along, may not seem to have much to do with money at the planning stage. But getting your kid to contemplate the question is a way to help him explore the connection. Ask questions such as: Are you using your own money for entrance fees, food, travel expenses, and equipment? Is that really how you want to spend your money? What will you have to economize on later if you do this now?

By now your teen may be earning more money from a part-time or summer job. Or maybe he has begun to receive funds from a trust fund, or has a generous aunt who occasionally slips him extra cash. Whatever his source of funds, it is wise to have him handle larger and larger shares of his spending budgets.

3. Helping to Focus on the Future

For 13-to-15-year-olds, the future isn't quite as far away as it once was. Though the developmental characteristics of this age include a focus on the self and only a vague awareness of the future, this is the time when helping kids dream big and expanding their vision of possibilities is critical.

Lifestyle Budgeting: A Practice Session

Give your kid a peek at his or her future with this lifestyle activity, which can be done at home or as part of a teen gathering.

1. First ask each teen to select a profession, job, or venture that will provide income by age 25. Make no judgments or comments about his selection.
2. Next have each teen search the Web for the average entry-level income for that choice. Visiting the job-finder website www.monster.com is often helpful in this exercise.
3. Have them list that income on a piece of paper (call it a balance sheet).
4. Now ask them to make some lifestyle choices. The sample budget on pages 102–103 will get them started. (Note that the numbers are national averages for a single person living alone and are hypothetical for the purposes of this activity. You can make them more meaningful by researching figures for your particular region of the country—or better yet, have the kids do that.)

Once the teens have made their selections, have them fill in the Budget Worksheet on page 105. For many kids this is a lightning-bolt insight. The very concept of "entry level" is alien to kids who have been taught by reality TV that stardom and wealth are instant attainments. This is the time to bring home a reality-based awareness about lifestyle choices and independence.

In the many workshops I run using a version of this activity, I have seen as many individual reactions and solutions as there are kids. One young woman who yearned to be an actress was startled to find that a first-year, entry-level actress *might* make $4,000 per year. When she saw that her lifestyle choices included owning a house and driving an SUV, she got very practical about what she would need to do if she really intended to pursue her dream (take a second job, rethink her material needs, start saving) and maintain her lifestyle choices. Of course, scaling back on the too-commonly shared desire for an SUV and a Neiman Marcus charge card become more rational choices at this point!

A young man who chose to pursue basketball as a career was stunned to see that entry-level salaries for NBA rookies average about $73,000 (for WNBA rookies this is only $30,000—can you spell *Title IX*?) and that only a very few players actually make as much as the megastars. He didn't give up his dream, but broadened his vision to consider owning a team, managing a team, being a coach, or being an agent. As he looked at what it would take to get where he wanted to go, he was able to make a connection between his career timeline and the lifestyle choices he would need to make.

Cool Jobs

Dolphin trainer

Mars Project engineer

Audio engineer

Marine biologist

Neurotechnology scientist

State senator

Television producer

Demographer

Hotel general manager

Botanist

Virtual-reality programmer

Magazine editor

Broadway theater manager

Vineyard manager

Digital cartoon animator

Currency trader

Family law attorney

Sierra Club lawyer

Grade-school teacher

College professor

Archaeologist

Astronomer

Detective

Sports agent

Sample Lifestyle Budget		
Housing	**Renter** (two-bedroom apartment) Average monthly rent:	$780
	Home Owner (costs include mortgage payment, property taxes, insurance, repairs) Average total monthly cost:	$1,173
Savings and Investment	**Minimum Investor** Monthly contribution:	$10
	Moderate Investor Monthly contribution:	$50
	Future Millionaire Monthly contribution:	$100
Food	**Thrifty Spender** (cooks at home, shops for sales, and sticks to a budget) Average monthly cost:	$325
	Moderate Spender (cooks at home, including some gourmet food, but occasionally splurges on a meal in a nice restaurant) Average monthly cost:	$450
	Big Spender (cooks gourmet and eats out often) Average monthly cost:	$800
Utilities	**Home Owner** (pays all monthly utilities, including gas, electric, fuel oil, water, and sewer) Average monthly cost:	$362
	Apartment Renter (pays electricity only) Average monthly cost:	$75
Health Care	**Copayments, services, and prescriptions** Average monthly cost:	$149
	Taking a pass on health care: Average monthly cost:	$0

Sample Lifestyle Budget		
Clothing	**Thrifty Spender** (shops at second-hand stores and sales and sticks to a budget) Average monthly cost:	$72
	Medium Spender (shops at The Gap, Express, Sears, and J.C. Penney) Average monthly cost:	$105
	Big Spender (buys designer clothes and shops at boutiques) Average monthly Cost:	$405
Transportation	**Public Transportation** Average monthly cost:	$50
	New Car (all vehicles financed zero down, 8% APR for 36 months; tax and license fees not included) Honda Civic, Monthly payment: Ford Explorer, Monthly payment: BMW 325 convertible, Monthly payment:	$470 $805 $1,148
	Used Car Nissan Sentra, Monthly payment: Acura Integra sports coupe, Monthly payment: BMW 323 sedan, Monthly payment:	$367 $586 $664
Car Operations	**Average Mileage Driver** (12,000 miles per year, with car insurance and repairs) Average monthly cost:	$320
	Heavy Mileage Driver (24,000 miles per year, with car insurance and repairs) Average monthly cost:	$375
Home Furnishings and Supplies	**New Home Furnishings** (Ikea style) Average monthly cost:	$157
	Used Home Furnishings (Goodwill purchases) Average monthly cost:	$107
	Raiding the Family Attic: Average monthly cost:	$0

Sample Lifestyle Budget

Telephone Service	**Talks a Little** Average monthly cost:	$60
	Talks a Lot Average monthly cost:	$90
Cell Phone	**Basic Monthly Service** Average monthly cost:	$43
	Bells and Whistles Average monthly cost:	$65
Cable TV	**Basic Monthly Service** (limited basic) Average monthly cost:	$22
	Every Conceivable Station (digital) Average monthly cost:	$78
Internet Service	**Basic Monthly Service** (dial-up) Average monthly cost:	$23
	Broadband Access (DSL) Average monthly cost:	$35
Entertainment	**Thrifty Spender** (rents videos, attends free concerts, frequents parks and libraries) Average monthly cost:	$87
	Medium Spender (goes to movies, local concerts, and sports events about once a week) Average monthly cost:	$148
	Big Spender (attends big-name concerts, big-ticket sports events, and the theater) Average monthly cost:	$292

Teens' Budget Worksheet		
Your Career	**Enter Monthly Net Salary**	$
Housing	Enter Monthly Mortgage or Rent	$
Savings and Investment	Enter Monthly Savings and Investment Contributions	$
Food	Enter Monthly Food Expenses	$
Utilities	Enter Monthly Utility Costs	$
Health Care	Enter Monthly Health Care Cost	$
Clothing	Enter Monthly Clothing Expenses	$
Transportation	Enter Monthly Transportation Costs	$
Car Operations	Enter Monthly Cost to Drive a Car (Enter $0 if you chose public transportation)	$
Home Furnishings and Supplies	Enter Monthly Home Furnishings Costs	$
Telephone Service	Enter Monthly Telephone Service Costs	$
Cell Phone	Enter Monthly Cell Phone Costs	$
Cable TV	Enter Monthly Cable TV Costs	$
Internet Service	Enter Monthly Internet Service Costs	$
Entertainment	Enter Monthly Entertainment Costs	$
1. Add up all of your monthly costs and enter the total in the box to the right.	**Total Monthly Costs =**	$
2. Now subtract your Total Monthly Costs from your Monthly Net Salary (first box). This amount is your Final Balance.	**Final Balance =**	$

Giving kids a chance to "practice their fantasies" in some reality-based way may feel like throwing cold water on their dreams. But not helping them to expand their visions in ways that allow them to attain real independence may cheat them of a full, secure, and satisfying future.

Lifestyle Budgeting: Real Life

The table on the opposite page is geared toward helping your teenager create a lifestyle budget for the present. Each category has two percentages, the first indicating what part of the budget the teen will be responsible for from her allowance and other income, and the second representing the percentage the parent will handle. Amounts for the allowance should be disbursed monthly or quarterly, depending on the teen's readiness to handle income. You may have to experiment a bit to figure out what her true readiness is—the goal is to have the teen handling a budget of a three-to-six-month duration by the time she's out of this stage of development.

Percentages listed are recommended only; you'll need to create your own formulas for your family. You may decide that in some of the categories you will contribute nothing; in some you will cover all of the expenses.

Clothing: This share percentage may change every six to twelve months. The more responsibility your kid has, the greater your responsibility not to give in to regular requests for extras. This is a learning exercise. If you want the right to splurge or to give a gift, do so, but acknowledge it as a special event, not a regular occurrence.

Entertainment: The simple act of asking your teen to estimate how many recreational activities and purchases he wants to engage in over the course of a one-to-three-month period and then tallying the total cost will be a revelation. With some kids, this is the easiest budget category to make into a learning experience. If your teenager wants to see three movies a month but spends his money on other things before he sees the third movie, he will have an instant "behavior has consequences" experience without you having to offer a single word of reproach. The learning, of course, will only happen *if you do not bail him out.* The point is to help him live with consequences when the stakes are not life-and-death. This is a lot easier when he is 13 than when he is 25 or 45.

Transportation: Even if you pay for 98 percent of transportation, being aware of the cost involved (gas, car maintenance, airfare, bus fare) is an impor-

Categories	Child / Parent	Amount per Month
Clothing	70/30	
Entertainment	70/30	
Transportation	20/30	
Education	10/30	
Food	20/30	
Hobbies	40/30	
Special Events	30/30	
Savings	50/30	
Philanthropy	90/30	

tant lesson for your teen. Asking her to contribute even 2 percent from her allowance puts the cost on her radar. And if it is transportation to ballet, riding lessons, or football practice, all the more reason to be aware of the costs.

Education: Both private and public schools, in an attempt to trim budgets, require families to cover an ever-wider range of school materials and activities. Again, you may cover 99 percent of all education costs for your teen, but letting her know the costs will clue her in to the investment being made in her future.

Food: This is another category in which the notion that "behavior has consequences" can be reinforced. Does all your son's money go to vending machines and french fries? If he isn't exercising some degree of control and moderation over his food habits, you can tie percentage increases in this part of the budget to improvements in his diet.

Hobbies: Whether your teenager plays soccer or collects comic books, an estimate of the expenses involved in these activities (including registration fees, trips, and purchases) will help her appreciate what it means to be able to invest money in a passion. If training for a place on the WNBA or a slot in the Winter Olympics is part of her dream, then uniforms, lessons, and coaches should be added into this category.

Special Events: You can't always anticipate a special event, but you can assume that there will be some, so it's possible to allocate a certain amount annually to cover the possibilities. And if this is the year of the bat or bar mitzvah, or some other rite of passage, factor that in as well.

Savings: Deducting a certain amount from each allowance payment is one way to get in the habit of saving. This should be nonnegotiable. If your kids have not yet learned to put savings aside by themselves, you may need to introduce them to the mechanism of the "automatic deduction" and simply withhold an agreed-upon part of the allowance to deposit in their bank accounts. Including them in the decision of where to place their savings is another way of teaching the idea that there are many ways to save. Does your child want to put the money into a CD or use a credit union? Contribute to a savings bank? Invest in Treasury bills? Asking teenagers to research where their money will make the most money is one way to get them engaged in the decision-making process.

Philanthropy: As we will see in chapter 9, philanthropy is a powerful way of connecting kids to something larger than themselves. By Stage Three, kids should be able to make enlightened choices about what to do with the money in their "giving jar." If your family experiences lean months throughout the year, you might suggest offering time in lieu of money.

By the time you and your teen tally up the total amount of her budget, it may look like an enormous amount of money—in fact it may be an enormous amount of money. But putting the numbers on paper is one way to reveal the hidden cost of family life—as well as give your teen some appreciation for the real choices you make in managing the larger family budget. If you are raising kids to be able to shepherd wealth responsibly, early practice is critical; if your family has been hit by a bad economy or an illness and you need everyone to pull together, shared information and collaboration is essential to helping kids feel secure and included in family solutions.

Often parents withhold information on the premise that it will only make kids feel anxious. This overlooks the quiet anxiety of kids whose fantasies create far more distressing realities than actually exist. Financial candor can and should be a part of daily family life, like parents' expectation of good manners or clarity about curfews.

Reactivating the Money Mentoring Team

These are the years when I often urge parents to "trade their kids." That is, it may be much easier for your daughter to hear things from her best friend's mom that she can't bear to hear from you—and likewise, your son's best friend may be more comfortable getting financial guidance in your house than in his own. Now is the time to reactivate your money mentoring team. (If you've just entered the book in this chapter, see page 28 for information about assembling a money mentoring team.)

Assuming the arrangement has worked out thus far, send your money mentors a note asking them to renew their agreement for another couple of years. (You may also want to add people who have come into your life who you think might be helpful.) Give them an update on your young teen and an idea of some issues and actions you hope they can help with. Remember that reciprocity is key here, and that your money mentor, just like you, may be busy and overwhelmed. Make sure you offer a gift certificate to dinner, an overnight stay for their kids at your house, or an equally meaningful gesture.

Here in Stage Three, you might ask the money mentor to:

- Share how his career has unfolded. Is he doing what he thought he would be doing? What does he enjoy most about his work? What does he wish someone had told him when he was 14?
- Take your teen to a meeting (a business meeting, city council meeting, club meeting) where adults are talking, planning, and considering ideas that relate to financial choices and decisions.
- Email your teenager a list of books that would make good reading and provide ideas about the future.
- Include your teen in a project to which she might make a small contribution.

This is also a stage in which you can suggest that your teens select their own money mentoring team. What do they want to learn and how will they recruit adults to teach them? Kids can be very effective in assembling their own mentors—and adults are often flattered to have been selected by teenagers. Whether it's the owner of a local business, the manager of a brokerage firm, or the executive director of United Way, your teen may actually be more successful than you in getting them to sign on as a money mentor.

Teens as Financial Futurists

Another strategy for helping teenagers to envision the future involves their friends. As part of a party or a sleepover, ask each teen to come prepared to create a "mural of the future." Give them each a giant piece of paper, markers, and lots of space to work in. Then ask them to draw three visions of the future (where they'll live, what they'll be doing, who they'll hang out with, what they'll be achieving): (1) a wild imagining of what might happen; (2) the scenario that's the most likely; and (3) a worst-case scenario (believe me, it's already in their heads—you're just putting it on the table, so to speak).

Once they have the picture complete, give them time to explain their depictions. Now ask them to revisit the mural and think about what it means financially:

- What will each scenario cost?
- Where will the money come from?
- How important is it for them actively build that future? How might they do that?
- What do they need to do to prevent the worst-case scenario from happening, and what might they do to ensure the best case?

4. Starting to Think Outside the Self

Whether she is aware of it or not, your child may already be shifting consciousness. Identifying with current issues, worrying about the plight of a friend, or identifying with a character in a film or book is part of this process. But getting her to think about money in a larger context means helping her see herself as part of the economic web of the community and of the nation.

Children of this age may be intuitively, if not consciously, aware that they and their friends help drive the economy. Indeed, they are likely to be quite aware that films, toys, high-tech products, clothes, sports equipment, and almost everything else they put their hands on are marketed to them aggressively—but that is not the same as understanding one's place in the economic web of the community. Seeing oneself as an *actor* as opposed to simply being acted upon is a vastly different perspective for the financial apprentice. One way to help your teen make this shift is to create a visual representation. You can complete the chart below with your teen to help illustrate the impact he already has on the financial life of the community.

Point out that the number of high schools and the dollars spent on constructing or renovating schools are directly related to how many school-aged students live in your town and how education for teens is prioritized in your community. You can also point out that tax dollars are spent to make sure that your son and his friends have access to summer recreation activities, a police force to provide security, and bike paths on which to ride safely. You might ask your daughter whether she's happy with the way her community regards the place of teenagers in the web—and if not, what would she like done differently?

Teens' Economic Impact

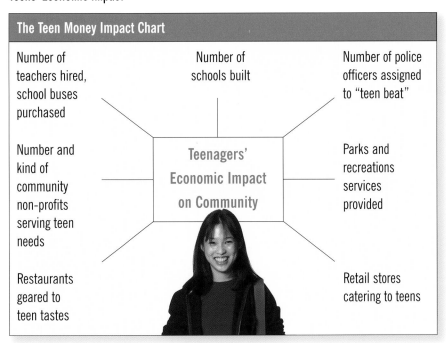

The Teen Money Impact Chart

Number of teachers hired, school buses purchased

Number of schools built

Number of police officers assigned to "teen beat"

Number and kind of community non-profits serving teen needs

Teenagers' Economic Impact on Community

Parks and recreations services provided

Restaurants geared to teen tastes

Retail stores catering to teens

Becoming aware of themselves in the wider context of a community can give kids a vital feeling of connectedness. You might build on this sensibility by taking a walking tour of your town or neighborhood and pointing out the parts of the community on which kids have an impact, such as:

- The number of schools built
- The number of school buses purchased

- The number of teachers hired
- The kinds of parks and recreational resources provided, such as a skateboard park, tennis courts, or a public swimming pool
- The success—or lack thereof—of stores that target teenagers as customers
- The size of churches and other houses of worship that are built
- The kinds of services offered by the local library

If the tour engenders a realization that kids are not having any significant impact—if the community is not putting money into services or facilities that make young peoples' lives better—this walking tour can trigger a sense of righteous outrage that will encourage some kids to become activists for their peers.

Youth Activism as an Element of Financial Literacy

Activism among young kids is a great way to help them achieve a sense of the world outside the self, asking "What does this mean for other kids in the community? In other countries?" Much has been changed by the force of a child's passion. Who can forget 10-year-old Samantha Smith, the little girl from Maine who had the moxie to write a letter to Yuri Andropov expressing her fear of nuclear war between his nation and the U.S. That letter put into play a whole series of events that took Samantha to the (then) Soviet Union to meet with Andropov. Today, Waging Peace (www.wagingpeace.org) is an internationally recognized nonprofit organization that emerged from the vision of this little girl.

Similarly, Kids Can Free the Children (www.freethechildren.org) was started by a 12-year-old in 1995. Craig Kielburger was searching for the comics in his local paper when he noticed an article about a young Pakistani boy who had been sold into bondage as a carpet weaver. Though the boy escaped, he was later murdered for speaking out against child labor. Moved by the boy's story, Craig rallied some friends and founded the organization Kids Can Free the Children.

Now a twentysomething young man, Kielburger has traveled worldwide to speak out in defense of children's rights, meeting with such figures as the Dalai Lama, Mother Teresa, and Pope John Paul II. The nonprofit organization he started has grown to involve more than a hundred thousand young people in over thirty-five countries. These young philanthropists have been responsible for the distribution of approximately one hundred thousand health and school kits and in excess of $2.5 million worth of medical supplies to needy families in the developing world. Kids Can Free the Children's advocacy campaigns have led Canada, Mexico, and Italy to pass legislation in order to better protect children from sexual abuse and exploitation. The organization has also lobbied corporations to adopt labels for child-labor–free products.

Your kids may not launch a worldwide organization, but helping them feel empowered by having an impact on other people's lives is an important step in their developing competence and self-worth. Kids who understand their part in the economic web of the world tend to make more thoughtful decisions for their own lives—as well as for the larger community.

Lauri Slavitt, a mom and a principal in a Silicon Valley foundation, relates this story:

Daniel (5) and Jordana (6) decided to start a business called The Key to Hope to help underprivileged children in the Bay Area. They began making special key chains in different designs. Each key chain takes an hour to make. They began by selling them to friends and family, but the key chains were beautiful and several people suggested they sell them at local supermarkets and community fairs. People were incredible. The kids ended up getting space at fairs and were allowed to solicit outside our local supermarket. Some people bought the key chains and then donated extra because they saw how earnest the kids were. The orders were coming in at such a rapid rate (special flags, individual designs, etc.) they decided to get up an hour early for school each day and do at least three at night. This business lasted for over one year and they made a total of $1,000. Most of the key chains sold for $3.00. They are now in the process of researching places to donate these monies.

Daniel and Jordana have begun "making a difference" well before adolescence, and there is a good chance their engagement with the community will have an inoculating effect against teenage cynicism. These kids have taken action, have been taken seriously, and are now engaged in a process that extends well beyond a simple empathic response to the needs of other kids.

Youth Investment Club

Forming an investment club is a great way for teens to learn the basics of wisely investing their money. See the following pages for instructions on how to start an investment club for teens.

How to Start an Investment Club for Teens

1 **Decide whether you want to start with real investments or have a "virtual" club.** In a virtual club you can use Monopoly money and work offline for a few months until the kids get the hang of the process. Even if you decide to "go real" immediately, there will still be a period of preliminary research, so you won't be putting money into stocks right away.

2 **Start with six or fewer teens.** Small numbers make learning easier, even though you won't accumulate as large a pool of cash to invest right away.

3 **Start the learning process: divide up assignments and have each member of the team report back.** Have one person read *The Motley Fool Investment Guide for Teens,* by David Gardner; have another visit www.better-investing.org (the website for the National Association of Investors Corporation [NAIC]); and another visit www.2020green.com (an interactive web-based curriculum of financial lessons). Discuss what each person discovered.

   Other good resources include:

   "So You Want to Start an Investment Club? A Plan to Get You Started":
   www.better-investing.org/articles/web/5184

   Go to www.about.com and type "investment clubs" in the "Find It Now" search box.

4 **Agree on a club name and start collecting examples of club rules, agreements, mission statements, and roles.** After reviewing what other people have done in their clubs, use one meeting to talk about the mission statement and procedures that would make sense for your club.

5 **Remember that this is a learning experience first**—making money comes after the learning!

6 **Once you have gathered information, you will need a partnership agreement among the club members.** There are over 115 NAIC chapters nationwide to help you start a club. To find a local chapter, call (877) ASK-NAIC or go to www.betterinvesting.org/articles/web/5287

7 Select a stockbroker who will make purchases for you. A grown-up will need to function as the legal representative, as children under 18 are not allowed to make purchases on their own.

8 Different clubs choose different ways to get started. Some invite experts to talk about different industries and companies (a graphic designer or animation artist might talk about what's new in the world of digital comics, for example, or an attorney might talk about what a partnership agreement is). Some clubs spend a lot of time reading and discussing articles from financial newspapers, magazines, and websites; others visit chat rooms and ask questions online (keeping in mind that telling the truth is not a guaranteed online activity!).

9 Designate an amount of money each member will contribute each month; $10 to $20 is an okay place to start. With six members contributing $20 each month, in a year the group will have almost $1,500 to invest—and a pretty good foundation for making their first investments. (Ideally, team members are each earning the $20 per month, not getting a handout from Mom or Dad.)

10 Hint to the club leader/grown-up: Your enterprising teens will be less likely to lose interest and drop out if they are given real responsibility and respect. However tempted you may be to make "good decisions" for them, resist the urge. To stay engaged, they must "own the club" and feel its importance.

11 Finally, be clear that this is not a club to join if the kids just want a cool summer activity. Like playing ball or learning a new instrument, becoming investment-savvy will take time and practice.

Caveat: The Dark Side of Financial Literacy

I would be remiss to talk about kids as though they are all children of June and Ward Cleaver, waiting eagerly for adult wisdom about issues of money and business. Money offers as much opportunity for wayward antics as any other part of kids' lives. And as the recent film (recommended for all parents) *Better Luck Tomorrow* portrays, superachieving young people with an abundance of resourcefulness and opportunity can be financially sophisticated and in a peck of trouble very easily.

Possible Concerns

The clever child who pushes the envelope to see what he can get away with (aka "the hustler"). These kids are often testing limits as they search for "the rules," or are just looking for something to do—in which case, helping them find ways to fill idle time is probably worth your while! Kids who are not shown clear ethics and boundaries relative to money may fall into habits that can get them into trouble with friends, employers, and the IRS later in life.

The independent child whose parents are sure everything is fine but don't push far enough to confirm that reality. Included in this group are parents who abdicate their role as overseer because they think, "My child is smart and knows what he's doing." Possibly the most dramatic example of this behavior was the Internet investing adventures of Jonathan Lebed, entertainingly reported by Michael Lewis in a February 2001 cover article for the *New York Times*.

Jonathan was described as a sullen, withdrawn 15-year-old who figured out how to reinvent himself online into a brash, confident Internet-savvy stockbroker. He and his friends mastered the art of the Internet message board, hyping stocks online, watching them climb in price, and selling at impressive (if overheated) profits.

Eventually, Jonathan accumulated over $800,000 in Internet stock profits, was investigated by the SEC (before whom his lawyer argued, fairly legitimately, that Jonathan's techniques were no different from those of many Wall Street analysts), and eventually was forced to return less than $300,000 in fines.

Michael Lewis leaves the reader to decide for him- or herself whether or not Jonathan did anything wrong. (That some of those analysts Jonathan's lawyer referred to have now been charged with crimes makes it a little less ambiguous.) But he does shed some light on how it happened:

Greg and Connie {Jonathan's parents} were born in New Jersey, but from the moment the Internet struck, they might as well have just arrived from Taiwan. When the Internet landed on them, it redistributed the prestige and authority that goes with a general understanding of the ways of the world away from the grown-ups and to the child. The grown-ups now depended on the child to translate for them. Technology had turned them into a family of immigrants. "I know, I know," Greg said, turning to me. "I'm supposed to know how it works. It's the future. But that's his future, not mine!"

Lewis makes the point that in abdicating knowledge of what Jonathan was actually up to at all hours, the parents provided ripe ground for his financial crimes. Indeed, computer-savvy kids who can reinvent themselves as anonymous adults online have ample opportunity to play out what otherwise might be adolescent antics with substantially higher risks and consequences.

The cynic. We don't have to exaggerate stories of depression, suicide rates, easy access to drugs, or early sex among kids today. Indeed, these are equal-opportunity problems among all income levels and ethnic groups. Another emerging concern is the tendency toward cynicism that arises when young people discover that the world, already confusing in the teen years, does not necessarily improve with the acquisition or control of money. In recent meetings with kids from around the U.S. as well as other countries, I've been struck by their awareness that money alone doesn't make the world a better place or make people any happier. To some extent, existential angst has always been a part of the adolescent and teen experience. But the more worldly teen of today, aware of (and not infrequently affected by) corporate greed and corruption, sees more tangibly and less existentially that pain and suffering are often unchanged and indeed may be exacerbated by great amounts of money. This can lead to an attitude that "all the money in the world doesn't seem to stop suffering, so if you can't change anything, why try?" This kind of lethargy comes from a level of depression and sadness that endless trips to the mall or a brand new car cannot fix.

Possible Solutions

Such hopelessness is surely not the province of all kids. But it is a state of mind I see often enough to pay close attention to. What can you do if you are living with a child who exhibits these signs? Here are four interventions you can try:

Take time. Unchallenged views grow insidiously. Lectures won't help—but conversation, real and often, can do wonders. Taking time to demonstrate the power of personal involvement—volunteering at a soup kitchen or participating in another activity that has a real effect on your community—can have an even stronger impact. Insist on finding a way to make a difference with your child. It is an active way to challenge youthful beliefs about how hopeless the world is.

Develop your own rotating internship program. If a child is disillusioned with the world, one role model may not be enough. Some kids require a *critical mass* of role models: one person making a difference may just be an anomaly, but ten role models constitute a reality shift. Enroll friends and colleagues for active duty. Friends who have responsibilities in community-based programs (the more grassroots, the better) or socially responsible businesses can each offer a day to host a child. If each of ten friends offers to host a child every month, each child will have a shot at seeing how at least ten people view the possibilities of changing the world. Your son or daughter may argue about the true impact these "role models" are making, but if so, they will have the very real experience of arguing with adults outside the family circle who can and will take them seriously. With any luck, one or more of these adults will connect with your child on a meaningful level.

Insist on action. This may sound obvious, but even the most world-weary child needs adult-imposed expectations. Perhaps the child has a great deal of despair about how little things matter, but allowing that worldview to be indulged without insisting the child test her assumptions does a disservice to her development. Children don't want to believe that nothing matters, but if you don't require involvement with something greater than themselves, they will be left to their own cynical beliefs.

Leverage peer power. Is there an event or activity you can invite your child's friends to participate in? If you arrange for ten kids to volunteer as a group at the local soup kitchen, or you recruit all your child's friends to throw a holiday party for a group of foster kids, you are harnessing the power of group think. While these "micro" actions will not solve the larger question of how to change the world, they will get kids talking and thinking about questions of micro vs. macro change—a vast improvement over change vs. no change.

Cynicism is a form of self-protection. Professed hopelessness gives kids an excuse to avoid risks. As grown-ups, we know that growth comes primarily through the process of taking risks, failing, learning, and trying again. Kids need to be drawn into experiences of risk-taking—and if not when they are young, when the stakes are lower, when? If children are not encouraged and pushed and bullied and lured into risk-taking by parents and grandparents, then by whom?

Many of us adults, worldly as we have become, may feel that there is legitimacy to a child's despair. One can hardly bear the front-page news of the day. Yet this makes it even more important to offer kids reasons for growing up, and instruction on how to employ wealth as a force for good. Adults usually have the counterbalancing knowledge that people who strive for a better world get both personal and existential satisfaction from the quest, and that indeed one person can make a difference. Kids need the adults in their lives to offer challenges to their half-formed ideas. It's part of your job as a grown-up.

Moving On

Closing this chapter with a cautionary word about the dark side of financial awareness is not meant to take anything away from the wonder of this stage of the financial apprenticeship. Taking steps toward independence is a form of primal optimism! It is a way the child has of saying "Yes! I can do this—I can be my own person." These teen years are a prime time for the emergence of a new independence. As we will see in the next chapter, an increased mastery of the Ten Basic Money Skills will provide teens with the self-confidence required to make a successful transition from child to young adult.

"You've got
to do your own growing,
no matter how tall
your grandfather was."

IRISH PROVERB

Chapter 6

Stage Four
Ages 16–18: Standing Tall

Breaking away now leads the confident teen to a posture of "standing tall." These are years in which teens begin to feel a genuine sense of self. They have less anxiety about the process of separation from their parents and are eager to pursue their visions of the future: leaving home for college, getting a full-time job, entering the military, or other life choices. One of the vehicles for this level of confidence is trusting one's self—and being trusted—to be financially responsible.

Throughout this book I emphasize that financial education is not just about the money. Financial competency is, in the best sense, a vehicle for kids to manifest their values, their character, and their substance. It's a means of demonstrating self-reliance and discipline—in short, a way of playing out the essence of who they are and who they will become.

The Life/Money Map
Stage Four / Ages 16–18

Social / Emotional Development	Appropriate Money Skills to Master
Has increased capacity for logical thought and planning	Actively saves, spends, invests
	Connects goals and saving
Preoccupied with acceptance by peer group	Experiences responsibility for self and others
Experimenting with independence	Able to talk about money and plan future
Confronts serious decisions about life	Understands money as power
	Can read a paycheck, do simple tax forms
	Shows developing capacity for economic self-sufficiency

Young people who are able to exercise judgment about using money in thoughtful and competent ways are not just kids with balanced checkbooks and a nest egg; they are kids who have made decisions about who they want to be and how they want to behave. Helping them use this final stage of the apprenticeship to polish the skills they have been working on over the years is one way to show your affection and respect for them.

Young people who have not learned to save, spend wisely, invest, handle debt and credit with self-awareness, and act philanthropically are more likely to have trouble leaving the nest, accrue debt soon after high school, and have chronic problems curbing the impulse to spend. These are the young adults who will spend a decade or more in a kind of "delayed apprenticeship," trying hard to acquire financial skills just when they need them most.

Personal Financial Safety Nets

By the time your children are juniors and seniors in high school, they should be focused on how to develop and manage their own financial safety nets. It's not necessary to scare your kids with visions of bag ladies and financial catastrophe to get their attention. But keep in mind that as they get ready to leave the house—either for college or that first full-time job—your kids are both vulnerable to the larger world and a part of it.

Teenagers are prey to every company that sees them as a credit-card target (college freshmen receive an average of eleven preapproved credit-card applications per month) or wants to establish early brand loyalty with them. These companies will make outrageous offers and promises to get your kids' attention. All this in an economy that already has a nasty habit of handing out rude surprises.

Economist Peter Passell maintains that "one of the of the most substantial changes in the U.S. economy over the last twenty years has been the shift of financial risk from the institution to the individual. This means *if you cannot manage your own financial security you will be out of luck.* That is, financial safety nets must now be woven by each of us to some extent. As many parents have a hard time doing this for themselves, it's tough to pass along to kids."

This lesson will be learned early among young people facing high unemployment rates as this book goes to press. According to Robert Reich, former secretary of labor, college graduates in 2003 faced the worst job market in twenty years. And from St. Petersburg, Florida, to New York City to Palo Alto, California, teens are finding that high unemployment rates mean that laid-off adults and older people unable to retire are filling the available jobs.

Not only are kids under pressure to become financially self-sufficient by virtue of fiscal policy, but for many kids, this is happening during a period in history when the job market is unwelcoming—and figuring out how to create a personal financial safety net is even more critical.

No Operating Instructions Included

Today's parents are not less capable or caring than their parents and grandparents. The fact is that the issues of kids and money *really are* more complex and challenging than ever. Before easy credit, mass communication, and family mobility, financial values were communicated through the extended family. Companies did not target kids as consumers so aggressively or have as many ways to do so, and parents did not compete in the same way with peers and media for their children's respect and attention.

In the '80s, these mounting pressures converged with a shift of attitude and policy that changed the financial landscape for parents and their kids. "Self-sufficiency" emerged as a value suggesting virtue and discipline. It started with welfare reform and inevitably trickled up to the everyday experience of working-class and middle-class people. Prior to the '80s, only a privileged few had easy access to the stock market, financial information, and financial products for saving and building wealth. In the '90s, the Internet and the rise of the "free-agent nation" fueled this growing regard for independence and self-management. The stock market and financial information became more accessible online—and 'round the clock. Numerous financial products and services became available, making it more critical than ever that individuals be financially literate in order to make choices they had never had to make before.

This shift of financial responsibility from institution to individual is, in a way, a true democratization of financial opportunity. But no longer can you let your retirement plans coast on autopilot while your employer (mis)manages your pension fund. You must choose between 401(k)s, IRAs, Roth IRAs, and a host of other financial options. And explaining it all to your children might be like trying to teach a foreign language you've never spoken yourself. As this new, more financially democratic—and complex—world has emerged, no one's been handing out operating instructions. Parents are left on their own to sort out their financial values and practices, much like trying to figure out those exasperating children's toys that used to come with four hundred pieces but no good diagrams to help you put them together.

In every part of a democratic society, *literacy matters*. To make a democracy—political or financial—effective, its members must know how to talk about, understand, and use the basic ideas and mechanisms of the culture.

Big Tasks for Stage Four

For this reason, the Big Tasks we discuss as part of each phase of development begin to take on more consequence in the fourth stage. They include:

1. The Ten Basic Money Skills: real-world applications
2. Making mistakes and making recovery: perhaps the greatest gift you can give your kids is the opportunity to take risks and make mistakes while the stakes are still low
3. Shifting from reliance on parents to reliance on self, including earning money and exploring entrepreneurship

I. The Ten Basic Money Skills: Real-World Applications

If you and your kids have been on track up to this point, they've been practicing the Ten Basic Money Skills in a low-risk/high-learning mode. (If you're just starting out, it's not the end of the world! You can still make great progress.) Learning iteratively and cumulatively, they may well be sick of hearing about the Ten Basic Money Skills—but they will surely never forget them!

In this final stage of financial apprenticeship, kids shift more and more from practice to application, from the lab to the real world. As they go off on more trips with friends (without you as their backup crew), prepare to go away to college and live on their own, fend for themselves in their first summer internship or part-time job, or take on more responsibility with family philanthropies or trust funds, they are now dealing with real life and its consequences.

The tasks and resources in this stage of the Life/Money Map raise the stakes for interaction with the larger world.

Common Teen Money Mistakes
The savings sinkhole
The credit morass
The collection obsession
Overcommitment
Lack of grace

2. Making Mistakes and Making Recovery

In a *New York Times* article about his life and career, Mark Levin, chief executive of Millennium Pharmaceuticals, said, "One of the most important things I have learned is that failure is good for you. People who do great things in life are those who went through a lot of adversity. I've made huge mistakes along the way."

And tech entrepreneur Jan Davidson, who started a software company (David Asssociates, creators of MathBlaster and other top-notch educational software) with $6,000 and an Apple II computer and sold it ten years later for over a billion dollars, was famous for asking her staff each day about the mistakes they had made. "If you don't make at least ten mistakes a day," she would tell them, "you aren't learning enough."

Who among us has not failed to get comparative bids for a big-ticket item and regretted our impulsiveness later? Or who has not bought something without checking track records or *Consumer Reports*, only to find out we have a lemon of a product? And when the small print on contracts and credit agreements is so small, we can easily miss information that comes back to haunt us later.

The years between 16 and 18 are prime years for great learning—and possibly the last low-stakes era in your kids' lives for making great learning mistakes. Perhaps the greatest gift you can give your kids is the opportunity to take risks and make mistakes. And when the mistakes show up, the operational question is not *what did you do wrong?* but *what have you learned?*

Here are stories shared by teens (and one aunt) in Independent Means programs that offer some pointed lessons:

The Savings Sinkhole.

Eighteen-year-old Sam was ready to buy a car. He had saved enough money to buy a used car and his parents, wanting him to be responsible for the car from the start, encouraged him to find a car he wanted and handle the purchase himself.

Sam looked up used car listings online and found a great buy, significantly less than the book price he'd expected to pay for the car he wanted. Thrilled at the savings he could demonstrate to his parents, Sam made contact with the seller, went to see the car, and learned that it had been in a slight accident, which accounted for the low price. The seller seemed very up-front and told Sam a repair for the accident was estimated to be in the order of $150. Sam liked the car and felt the repair was within his budget—and still left him with a little money left over. So, without further consultation with his parents, he made the deal and took possession of the car.

Shortly after this, Sam took the car to a mechanic to get the repair made. To his chagrin and mortification, the mechanic informed him that the repair would be extensive and would cost roughly ten times what the seller had estimated. Sam's eagerness (and good intention) to save money was undermined by his failure to do his homework *before* making a significant purchase. Similarly, had he checked in with his parents (or looked up used-car-buying guidelines on the Web), they might have insisted he get the car inspected *first*.

His parents, hoping he would not forget this experience, advanced him the money for the repair, but insisted he pay them back over time. Quite wisely, they felt that bailing him out would allow him to forget the consequences of his action far sooner than being reminded every time he made a payment to them.

Ironically, many kids absorb the saving-money lesson eagerly. Being able to say, "But *Mom*, look at the money I saved!" often seems like a great way to gain approval while still getting what they want. The problem with this, as we all know, is that the advertising industry has become very clever about how they help people save money while spending it at the same time. Young girls who shop exclusively at discount stores will say, "But Dad, I saved a couple of hundred dollars today," conveniently ignoring the reality of having spent $250 to do that.

The moral of this story for parents is to be wary of focusing only on saving. If financial education for kids is limited to an emphasis on saving at the expense of the other nine skills, kids may seek approval for saving while spending their way into a pile of debt!

Financial savvy for kids consists of a balanced understanding of how each of the skills supports the others. If you are frustrated by your teen's spending habits, listen to how he talks about saving. If his savings account doesn't show real growth, his checking account is not balanced, and the word *budget* isn't part of his vocabulary, you may not be spending enough time on money messages that go beyond exhorting him to save.

In this case, Sam's parents showed strength in helping him learn from his savings adventure and expand his notion of financial responsibility.

The Credit Morass

Seventeen-year-old Andrea received a credit card application in the mail. She had an active babysitting practice and cleared a few hundred dollars a month. She had saved her money regularly and thought of herself as pretty reliable. She was getting ready to go away for a summer program at a college in the next state and talked her grandmother into cosigning for a card "for emergency purposes." Because Andrea was usually very responsible, the grandmother agreed, with the proviso that Andrea would have to pay for anything that was not absolutely of an emergency nature and would have to cover that balance each month.

Perhaps the greatest gift you can give your kids is the opportunity to take risks and make mistakes. And when the mistakes show up, the operational question is not *what did you do wrong?* but *what have you learned?*

Andrea's program schedule included a number of field trips each week. Away from home and in an environment of adventure with new friends who seemed to have lots of money to spend, Andrea found many opportunities for using her new credit card. Within three weeks her balance was well over $400 and none of the charges could be termed of an emergency nature. By the end of the month she already knew she could not pay off the whole balance, so she paid just a part of it instead. She could, she reasoned, start to economize and on average would be in a better position to pay off the whole balance before the end of the next month.

But the next month brought more field trips, and the pressure to keep up with her friends as they ate, shopped, and enjoyed their outings meant that Andrea's balance kept growing—even though her ability to pay didn't. By the time she returned home, Andrea's credit card was maxed out and she was facing both interest fees and her grandmother's disappointment.

But Andrea's grandmother wisely knew that this was a time to learn, not a time to aggravate the situation by letting her get deeper in debt and ruin her credit rating. Andrea got her first lesson in the art of restructuring debt. First, her grandmother paid off the credit card, then created a new "account" in which Andrea now owed her instead of the credit card company. (She didn't cancel the credit card, just put it aside for a while.)

Andrea had to sign a contract with her grandmother, agreeing to pay off the debt over a period of months. Andrea's grandmother lowered her interest rate from the 18 percent the credit-card company was charging to 6 percent. It wasn't nearly what a real credit card would cost, but it did remind Andrea of the cost of credit. There was no charging available under the new contract with her grandmother. If Andrea wanted a new CD or a pair of jeans, she had to have the cash first before making the purchase.

It took nine months before Andrea was free of debt. By then she was just a few months away from her first semester of college. Instead of forbidding her to have a credit card, now her grandmother hoped she had learned her lesson about credit and how easy it is to get out of control. It worked: Andrea became a crusader among her friends, and the credit card became a tool for emergencies, not a recreational vehicle. Andrea's new behavior arose from her grandmother's cool-headed commitment to helping her learn from her mistake rather than simply imposing punishment.

The Collection Obsession

Alex had started to collect stamps when she was just a little girl and her mother's best friend gave her a plate block of beautiful stamps. As she grew older, she became entranced by the pictures and the stories behind the stamps, as well as their investment value. Relatives gave Alex stamps for birthdays and Chanukah, and part of her allowance went to buying stamps every week. As she got older, she attended fairs and shows where she traded for more stamps. By the time she was in high school her collection was extensive and quite valuable.

For a long time, Alex's parents encouraged her passion for the stamps. How bad could this be? She was investing in a valuable collection and learning a lot about history, science, and geography at the same time. But by the time she was a junior in high school her passion had become an obsession. She was spending more and more time studying the stamps, and more and more money on her collection. Finally, a stamp came on the market that was way beyond her resources and she knew it was more than her parents could pay as well. But she really wanted the stamp and was determined to get it by hook or by crook. She began to steal money from her parents. When she had enough money, she purchased her beloved stamp and hid it in a notebook in her room. But getting the stamp did little to stem her hunger for the tiny works of art. She wanted more. She continued to steal and buy more stamps.

Eventually, of course, she was caught. Confronting her, Alex's parents gave her a tough choice: sell the collection to pay them back and gain some perspective or diversify her interests, selling part of her collection to pay them back and leaving the rest of the collection in safekeeping with them for a year.

Alex was angry and ashamed for several months, but her parents did not back down. Finally, she chose option B and sold part of her collection to pay back her parents. The forced vacation from her passion gave her space to gain a little perspective.

Even though we normally applaud the emerging passions of young people, it's important to be aware when they spill over into less positive behaviors and need to be redirected. Alex wasn't a pathological thief, but she was isolated from friends and other interests. Her passion had elicited so much approval throughout her childhood that it was hard to give it up. With the help of her family she has expanded her friendship circle and diversified her portfolio of interests.

Overcommitted

At 16, Phil had a part-time job working for a company owned by one of his dad's best friends. Though he only worked twelve to fourteen hours a week, he was also president of his class, a once-a-week volunteer at the local humane society, and the center of attention among a great group of friends. He managed to keep his grades up, though they were not as high as his parents thought they might be if he were not so busy.

Still, they felt he had a well-rounded life and trusted him to make good decisions about priorities. Phil's juggling act was a little precarious, but worked reasonably well until his employer offered him a bonus to help out on a special project that would last for three months and for which he could earn an extra $500 per month. He agreed and the juggling act went into high gear.

It wasn't long before Phil's mother began to notice that her son was dragging in the morning and irritable when he got home each night. His friends began to complain they didn't see him any longer and in order not to alienate them he pushed himself to see them later in the evening. Not surprisingly, in the third month of this hectic schedule, Phil caught a cold—but it turned into a serious virus that landed him in the hospital.

Phil's parents were proud of their son and pleased he was exhibiting such a strong work ethic, but they realized that he was not learning to set boundaries and that his desire to make extra money was not teaching him good habits so much as it was teaching him that doing it all required pushing beyond reasonable limits. Rather than issue an edict about what he could and couldn't do, they decided to work with him to set boundaries. Illness had caught Phil's attention and his parents were able to use the insight that came from crisis to help him think about how he wanted to live.

Neither Phil nor his parents wanted him to be less engaged with work, friends, or education—the question was how to manage his enthusiasms in a way that didn't undermine his health. Phil noticed that in his very busy schedule there was little room or time for himself. He decided that he had to clear his plate every week to have at least half a day all to himself with no claims from the external world. In the beginning this affected his bottom line, and the fact that his savings account was not growing at the pace he had grown used to troubled him. But as the months progressed and his "time-outs" helped him grow both stronger and more peaceful, Phil could see that being more purposeful about making money and spending time with others would probably pay off. By letting Phil make this discovery himself, his parents didn't make him feel less powerful; they just gave him some needed perspective.

It's worth noting that futurist Faith Popcorn has identified a new phenomenon emerging that she calls "free-range kids." These are children who are *not* overscheduled with play dates and professional classes. These kids, like children in earlier generations, are allowed—even encouraged—to spend time "doing nothing" and devising their own forms of entertainment. As a financial skill, what I like about this new trend is that we know that young people who are required to develop their own resourcefulness are better off financially. If your kids are burdened with busy schedules, it's worth exploring whether a more "free-range" kid might be a happier kid.

Flip Open

3. How to get paid what you are worth	4. How to spend wisely	5. How to talk about money	6. How to live a budget
Ask your child to list three skills or talents he has and what he thinks a fair fee is for those skills. Have him compare his estimates to information he finds on the Web to see if his estimate is high or low.	**Give a lesson on tipping:** when and how much.	**Discuss the family estate plans:** talk about wills and other legal documents your kids should know about in case of an emergency.	**Explain the concept of a pension.** Ask your teen to figure out how many ways he can save for a pension fund.
Introduce the concepts of equity, salary, wages, commission, and bonuses as ways of getting paid. Ask your teen which she thinks are the best forms of payment.	**Take your teen** with you to buy the next family car, computer, entertainment center, or other big-ticket item, then let her research, choose, and go with you to purchase the next big item after that.	**Discuss dating etiquette** and how your son or daughter can handle the issue of who spends money for what on dates.	**Give your teen three hypothetical annual incomes** of $23,000, $65,000, and $150,000. Ask her to create a budget for each lifestyle. Remind her to figure in taxes, savings, and philanthropy in each of the budgets.
Role-play the pay negotiation process with your kids *before* their next job interview.	**Give your teen a subscription** to *Consumer Reports* for Valentine's Day.	**Ask your teen to list her top five money worries** and then ask her to come up with a plan for reducing her anxiety.	**Ask not** "What kind of lifestyle do you want to live?" but "What kind of person do you want to be?" How do you budget for that?
	If you let your kid have a cell phone, ask him to recommend three different billing options, showing which is the most cost-effective.	**Have your teen write budgets** for three to five rites of passage such as a prom, wedding, or other celebration.	
A website for teens looking for a job: www.teens4hire.org Informational website of *Sound Money*, a National Public Radio program focusing on personal finance and the economy: www.soundmoney.org/	Teen Consumer Scrapbook of informational articles: www.wa.gov/ago/teenconsumer Learn about the holistic worldview of the LOHAS Consumer, comprising environmental concerns, human health, and human rights: www.lohasjournal.com	A PBS Online NewsHour website for students with information about savings, jobs, investing, entrepreneurship, and funding a college education: www.pbs.org/newshour/on2/money.html The NEFE Teen Resource Bureau: www.ntrbonline.org	*Prince Charming Isn't Coming: How Women Get Smart About Money,* Barbara Stanny *My Budget Planner for Teens (Ages 10-18):* www.womens-finance.com/store/mbpteens.shtml

When kids make financial

mistakes the operational question is not,

What did you do wrong?

It is, What have you learned?

7. How to invest	8. How to exercise the entrepreneurial spirit	9. How to handle credit	10. How to use money to change the world
To remind your teen what a bond is, you can explain that the word comes from the early English word band, meaning a fastening. In investing terminology, a bond implies that one is bound to repay an obligation.	**Take your kid** to an Inc. 500 (or other) conference for entrepreneurs.	**If you help your teen get a credit card,** be sure to show her how to safeguard against credit card fraud.	**Give your teen a subscription** to YES! magazine.
Set up a time for your kid to meet with your financial advisor to talk about what an advisor's role is.	**Send your teen an email** reminding her that entrepreneurs are people who make ideas happen with resourcefulness and ingenuity. Tell her that entrepreneurs start non-profits, work in large companies, and may be found on the staff of a church as well as in the world of science and technology.	**Ask your teen** to find out what a "teaser rate" is.	**Ask your kid to list three causes that matter to her.** Ask her to create a plan for supporting those causes.
Take your teen to an annual meeting.		**Make sure that you charge interest when you loan money to your kids.** It can be a low rate, but you want to remind them that borrowing costs money.	**Ask your teen to identify and investigate** which of the companies behind his favorite brands actually practice socially responsible business. Ask him to be specific about what makes them socially responsible.
Give your teen a subscription to the GreenMoney Journal.	**Remind your teenager** of things he does that are entrepreneurial in nature.	**Have your kid check his credit rating** (if applicable).	

The Motley Fool Investment Guide for Teens: 8 Steps to Having More Money Than Your Parents Ever Dreamed Of, Tom and David Gardner	*Losing My Virginity: How I've Survived, Had Fun, and Made a Fortune Doing Business My Way,* Richard Branson	*Credit Cards and Checks (Earning, Saving, Spending),* Margaret Hall	Nonprofit organization dedicated to promoting ecological and social action: www.yesmagazine.org
Women of the Street: Making It On Wall Street in the World's Toughest Business, Sue Herera	*Our Wildest Dreams: Women Entrepreneurs Making Money, Having Fun, Doing Good,* Joline Godfrey	*Electric Money: How the Computer Revolution Has Radically Transformed the Way We Save, Spend, and, Think About Money:* PBS video, available through www.amazon.com	Software that maximizes your tax deductions by providing fair market value of donations to charity: www.itsdeductible.com
		A "consumer credit resolution" site for debtors: www.getdebtfree.com	www.youthnoise.com

The Ten Basic Money Skills: Real-World Applications

If you and your kids have been on track up to this point, they've been practicing the Ten Basic Money Skills in a low-risk/high-learning mode. (If you're just starting out, it's not the end of the world! You can still make great progress.) Learning iteratively and cumulatively, they may well be sick of hearing about the Ten Basic Money Skills—but they will surely never forget them!

In this final stage of financial apprenticeship, kids shift more and more from practice to application, from the lab to the real world. As they go off on more trips with friends (without you as their backup crew), prepare to go away to college and live on their own, fend for themselves in their first summer internship or part-time job, or take on more responsibility with family philanthropies or trust funds, they are now dealing with real life and its consequences.

The tasks and resources in this stage raise the stakes for interaction with the larger world.

Basic Money Skill		
	1. How to save	2. How to keep track of money
Actions: 16–18 Years	**Introduce the concept of a credit union** and give your child the option to join one. **Send an email** that says "The quickest road to a good credit rating is a good savings record." **Suggest that your child set a savings goal** for a down payment on a house and calculate what she needs to save each month for the next ten years to attain it.	**Now is the time to have an annual budget for your child.** Review it quarterly. **Choose a time** of year that is both a rite of passage and occasion for celebration to review the annual budget. **If your teen has a part-time job, have him fill out a tax return form.** Help, but do not do it for him. **Ask your teen to fill out her own college financial aid forms.** Let her interview you for the information she needs. **Provide an overview of the family financial situation.** Make sure your teen understands her part in the overall family plan.
Resources	An interactive Web-based curriculum of financial lessons: www.2020green.com *Think Single: The Woman's Guide to Financial Security at Every Stage of Life,* Janet Bodnar	*Money Matters for Teens Workbook: Age 15–18,* Larry Burkett An interactive website "for kids who want to get a head start on their financial future": www.italladdsup.org Personal finance software: www.intuit.com/products_ services/personal_finance/ quicken/

Financial competency is a way

for kids to manifest their character;

a way of playing out the essence of

who they are and who they will become.

Forgetting Grace

Though it's not listed as one of the Ten Basic Money Skills, I have come to feel that gratitude should surely be addressed in that vein. The aunt who sent me the following email articulates a level of consternation that often arises in families in which there is a disconnection between financial savvy and character.

She wrote: "I have four nephews and nieces, ages 14 to 18, who live about two thousand miles from me, so I rarely see them at Christmas, though they know me well and we spend time together during the summer. Each year I spend time and money selecting gifts I think they will really like. And their parents (my siblings) tell me they *do*. But of the four, only my 15-year-old niece reliably sends a thank-you note. I'm tempted just to buy for her next year. Am I being unreasonable?"

The other three children in the family are clearly making a big mistake with their aunt—and patterns being what they are, will likely repeat this mistake, possibly in areas where the stakes are even higher (a mentor who gives time or opens doors is not properly thanked and decides to stop providing support, or a client who is taken for granted decides to purchase services or products elsewhere) if an intervention is not made soon. If kids think they are *entitled to* presents, just because it's their birthday or a holiday of gift giving, they won't connect giving thanks with receiving gifts. In the mind of an entitled child, these are not *gifts* in the real sense of the word, but *loot*.

Resources for Helping Kids Develop Grace

Goops and How to Be Them: A Manual of Manners for Polite Children, Gelett Burgess and Barbara Ross

Oops! The Manners Guide for Girls, Nancy Holyoke

Be The Best You Can Be: A Guide to Etiquette and Self-Improvement for Children and Teens, Robin Thompson

Tiffany's Table Manners for Teenagers, Walter Hoving

How Rude! The Teenagers' Guide to Good Manners, Proper Behavior, and Not Grossing People Out, Alex J., Ph.D.

365 Manners Kids Should Know: Games, Activities, and Other Fun Ways to Help Children Learn Etiquette, Sheryl Eberly

Madeline Says Merci: The Always Be Polite Book, John Bemelmans Marciano

Short of cutting off the supply to make a point, what can this aunt do? She has a number of options for helping her nieces and nephews develop grace and money skills that will serve them well over the course of their lives:

- Next year, her presents can be books that speak to the issues of gift giving and giving thanks.

- When she sees them in the summer, she can initiate conversations about gift giving, including what giving and receiving symbolizes and how the exchange can be honored.

- To offer a slightly different perspective on the event, she can suggest that next year they all exchange gifts they make rather than buy.

- She can speak to her sister or brother. One parent I know insists that the kids write short thank-you notes as they unwrap gifts. One gift can't be unwrapped until the previous note is completed (and yes, he does allow email thanks). Though this approach is a little extreme, the point is certainly made.

For More information about Camp $tart Up, visit www.DollarDiva.com

A few years ago, we introduced Business Etiquette sessions at Camp $tart-Up, a summer program for teen women who want to learn how to turn an idea into a business or philanthropic enterprise. I wasn't sure how the teens would react to these classes, so I was somewhat surprised when they turned out to be among the favorite classes at the camp. It seems that a lot of young people are in fact embarrassed to have bad manners and are eager to learn how to act more grown-up and sophisticated.

Another option this aunt has is to use her time in the summer to be an etiquette role model, not only on thank-you notes but also on the basics of using utensils properly at the table, introducing and being introduced, shaking hands, and the myriad other "etiquette skills" that are not routinely taught. When kids don't acquire these skills it is often because no one took them time to teach them.

Why do I call gratitude and proper etiquette another money skill? Because at the heart of good financial relationships is a respect for reciprocity. Whether appreciation for a job well done (labor well rewarded, or a higher price for a beautifully crafted product) or an acknowledgment of a fair exchange, kids who grow up with a more complex appreciation for giving and receiving will have a healthier attitude about money in general.

Whether appreciation for a job well done (labor well rewarded, or a higher price for a beautifully crafted product) or an acknowledgment of a fair exchange, kids who grow up with a more complex appreciation for giving and receiving will have a healthier attitude about money in general.

The "mistakes" chronicled above are all acts committed and, for the most part, corrected by teens themselves. But key to each of the stories is the engagement of a parent or other adult who—without punishing, castigating, or shaming—helped guide the young person through the learning opportunity associated with the mistake. As in any good learning experience, insight comes from the discourse, from the caring respect and involvement of a person who has the best interests of the teen at heart and acts on the profound conviction that the child wants to be a better person.

3. Shifting to Reliance on Self

The beauty of a conscious financial apprenticeship is that it provides a low-risk, sheltered environment for practicing the Ten Basic Money Skills. This final stage is a launching pad for moving out of the shelter into a larger arena. Whether training for sports, a school play, or college entrance exams, a time comes when the practice shifts to performance. So it is with one's financial apprenticeship. The most important Big Task for parents is to help their children master the lessons of Stages One, Two, and Three before they are in fact on their own. And essential to developing self-reliance and becoming self-sufficient is the ability to earn money, whether through employment or entrepreneurship.

Part-Time Work for Teens

First, the facts: laws regulating employment of minors vary among states and U.S. territories. But according to the U.S. Department of Labor's Fair Labor Standards Act (FLSA), the minimum age for employment is 14. In addition, the FLSA prohibits the employment of minors in hazardous work (excavation,

Books to Inspire Emerging Entrepreneurs

Growing a Business, Paul Hawken

Body and Soul: Profits with Principles, Anita Roddick

Steve Jobs: Thinks Different, Ann Brashares

A Garlic Testament: Seasons on a Small New Mexico Farm, Stanley G. Crawford

Ben & Jerry's: The Inside Scoop, Fred "Chico" Lager

Losing My Virginity: How I've Survived, Had Fun, and Made a Fortune Doing Business My Way, Richard Branson

Our Wildest Dreams: Women Entrepeneurs Making Money, Having Fun, Doing Good, Joline Godfrey

driving, and the operation of many types of power-driven equipment). There are, however, exceptions to FLSA restrictions. For example, minimum age requirements do not apply to minors employed by their parents or guardians. Young people of any age may also deliver newspapers; perform in radio, television, movie, or theatrical productions; and baby-sit or perform other minor duties around a private home.

The pressing question from parents is whether or not kids *should* work (presuming they have a choice, of course, as not all families have that luxury). That question has been studied exhaustively and though the studies are often conflicting, there does seem to be a real indication that the number of hours a high school student works each week is a significant factor in her academic performance and personal growth. That is, while working *more* than fifteen hours a week seems to correlate with lower grades and impaired behavior, kids who work *less* than fifteen hours a week in school-based internships and job programs seem to acquire real benefits. Anecdotally, I can report that the young people I have encountered as interns, full-time employees, and even summer-camp attendees exhibit more sophisticated life skills and judgment if they have had some early work experience in their formative years.

As with so much in child development, whether or not and how much your particular child should work will vary from family to family. But the value of early experiences in getting and keeping a job and managing earned money are valuable enough that, within a reasonable set of guidelines, I highly encourage teens to work—particularly during summer months. As a parent, here are some of the questions to ask and the parameters to put in place to ensure that work is a healthy choice for your child:

Will the work reduce the number of hours of sleep the teen gets? It is commonly accepted now that teens really do need more sleep. Adding responsibilities that reduce your child's sleep significantly is probably not a good idea. If the job is a priority, what other activities might be cut down to make sure that sleep isn't one of them?

Is it safe? Is transportation to and from the workplace convenient and safe? Do you know the company and have you met the employer? No child wants his mom and dad to show up at work like it's the first day of kindergarten, but as a parent you want to at least have an idea with whom your son and daughter is now spending time.

What's the cost of work and does it outweigh the benefits? If a uniform or particular style of dress is required that costs more than the child makes each week, you need to be aware of that and help your kids make a cost/benefit analysis of whether this job makes sense.

Is your child being paid fairly? Kids are often given "go-fer" jobs that give them great work experience in exchange for relatively low pay—we used to call this "paying dues." But if it appears to you that your child with exceptional skills (a young computer programmer, for example) or talent (great writing skills) or just incredible energy is being used excessively without proper compensation, you'll need to talk with her about what's fair and how to advocate for herself with her employer.

Is your child meeting people, networking, or learning skills that will make a difference later in life? Keep in mind that there may be more to a job than meets the eye. I remember a few unbelievably tedious jobs that I endured as a teen only because I wanted the paycheck enough to put up with the dull work. Only years later was I able to see just how terrific my employers had been and how much I learned about the importance of reliability and discipline. In retrospect I would not have given up those jobs for anything—but it might have been a hard call at the time! In fact, I once wrote a column on the value of a boring summer job, making the case that being imaginative enough to make more of that job than appears possible will give you an edge throughout your career.

Why is your child doing this particular job? Is it his choice? Is it something you set up? Did he just fall into it easily? While job-hopping became more acceptable during the dot-com boom, you don't want to encourage too-frequent job changes. On the other hand, these are your kid's years to experiment and try new things. Evaluate whether the job he's chosen is right for him.

Self-Employment and Entrepreneurship

I often use entrepreneurship as a means of engaging kids in an exploration of money and business. Rarely do I portray making money as an end in itself. Instead, I find it far more effective to emphasize that entrepreneurship is a vehicle for achieving independence. Although teen interest in entrepreneurship is very high, in truth I am not terribly interested in having millions of kids start their own businesses. I want them to focus on their education. However, gaining the *skills* and *understanding* of entrepreneurship is valuable to kids for a host of reasons:

- Whether or not your kids ever start their own businesses, it is true that every employer seeks self-motivated, self-managing employees. While once shunned by many large corporations, the entrepreneurial employee is now in high demand.

- Lawyers, doctors, accountants, and many other professionals who function as sole practitioners discover quickly that a lack of business skills can undermine the pursuit of their chosen profession. As one teenage participant at Camp $tart-Up said to me, "I don't really want to have my own business; I want to be a lawyer. But eventually I may want to start my own practice." (Smart girl—she's planning ahead!)

- If their job options are limited, kids will still have an option—they can figure out a way to employ themselves.

- Exploring entrepreneurship is an excellent means of introducing the language and concepts of money into "real life." Balance sheets, profit and loss, budgeting—all these concepts may be understood more readily in the exciting realm of "having my own business."

- Finally, there is the relevance of introducing one of the most important paths to building wealth. A number of books (The Millionaire Next Door and Rich Dad, Poor Dad being among the most successful) have helped families understand how important it is to help kids see beyond the collection of a monthly or weekly paycheck to the building of wealth over the long term.

Teaching kids about equity, or company ownership, first through the very concrete mechanism of a real company and later through investing in other companies, is one way to help kids see themselves as their own best security blanket. While many families encourage their kids to get an education and take a "secure job," in 2003 the number of unemployed people in the U.S. was 8.8 million, the highest in a decade, while the overall number of jobs had slipped to a three-year low. Clearly, the next generation will need to pursue wealth building as a means of financial security, not just rely on paychecks from a so-called secure job.

In each stage of the financial apprenticeship I have encouraged the development of entrepreneurial skills, in part because it is a developmentally effective activity and in part because kids are often simply curious and intrigued by the notion. Indeed, in the last five years the number of local and national business-plan competitions for young people has exploded. From a Venture Capital Competition for high school students affiliated with the Haas School of Management at Berkeley (www.haas.berkeley.edu/yeah/venture.htm) to the YoungBiz Competition (www.youngbiz.com), opportunities for kids to practice turning moneymaking ideas into moneymaking ventures are growing.

Every year Independent Means offers a DollarDiva Business Plan Competition for teen girls(www.DollarDiva.com) and summer camps that offer the opportunity to create a business plan for a company. For many kids this is their first opportunity to work out a balance sheet and begin to think through the process of creating a venture that will make money. Recent plans from teens have included:

"Make a Difference" by Larissa Curlik of New Jersey: an online periodical that features the changes that teens are making in their communities and throughout the world. "Make a Difference" also provides the inspiration and ideas teens need to start their own volunteer projects or to get involved in programs already running in their communities and schools.

"Her Place" by Amanda Graves of Arizona: a photographic studio and digital imaging business created to sell a line of digital art that conveys the empowerment of teenage women.

Resources for Creating a Business Plan

www.sba.gov/starting_business/special/young.html

www.YoungBiz.com

www.DollarDiva.com, National Business Plan Competition

The Young Enterpreneur's Edge, Jennifer Kushell

The Lemonade Stand: A Guide to Encouraging the Entrepreneur in Your Child, Emmanuel Modu

50 Great Businesses for Teens, Sarah L. Riehm

"Signatures of Memories" by Genika Green of Louisiana: a manufacturing business that specializes in making and selling unique autographed pillows for both wholesale and retail customers. The pillows are designed to preserve memories of special events such as high school graduation, proms, and birthdays.

"Senior Link" by Victoria Sehgal of New York: a place where senior citizens are introduced to and benefit from the world of information technology. "Senior Link" uses knowledgeable teenagers to teach seniors the valuable computer skills they need to help with their daily lives.

"myDiaryBook.com" by Michelle Wong of Washington: an Internet application designed to deliver unique, online diary management services to its customers.

You'll notice that most of the plans either cater to or involve teens—their creators are intimate with and understand their markets. Now, often these first efforts are, as you might imagine, a little unpolished. Sometimes the kids make big assumptions that cannot be supported; sometimes they simply don't do the math correctly. Their counselors and coaches point out issues that need to be addressed, and when the kids correct their mistakes they learn valuable financial lessons.

We get very excited about the mistakes these kids make. "This," I remind them, "is the best opportunity you will get to make big mistakes and have the stakes be so low. Making errors in your business plan when you are 30 or 40 means there will be real consequences—from cash-flow problems to Chapter 11. But when you are just practicing, the errors you make are learning errors, not the end of the world."

So if you have a champion Girl Scout–cookie salesperson in your family, or a child who always has an idea for a business, help channel that wonderful energy right into a business plan—another exercise in financial skill building (see sidebar on facing page for resources on how to create a business plan).

Self-Reliance and the Extended Family

Throughout this book I refer often to parents and their kids. It should go without saying that financial education of the next generation is a collective responsibility all adults share. Whether you are a grandparent or close family friend, a godfather or an aunt, it is your obligation to help the kids in your life become both money-wise and financially competent.

One night after I had given a talk to clients of an asset-management firm in Colorado, I was approached by a couple who explained, "We did a very poor job of raising our own children to be financially responsible. Now we see what terrible money habits they are instilling in their own children. We don't want to meddle in our children's lives, but we're terribly concerned about what will happen to our grandchildren."

I asked them to consider what they might do if, while visiting their grandchildren, they noticed that the kids had wandered into the road and their parents weren't taking any action about the behavior. Would they feel they were meddling to pull the kids out of the street and into safety? The couple immediately said, "Of course not."

Without *someone* intervening, children who miss their financial apprenticeship are vulnerable to the worst of life's surprises. Financial literacy is economic self-defense and we all have responsibility to function as money mentors, guides, and "consultants" to the next generation. When you perceive opportunities to reinforce a young person's inclination toward self-reliance, go ahead and take advantage of the moment. We each remember an adult (teacher, friend, special aunt or uncle) who made a difference in our lives. Do not be afraid to be that person for someone else. And if you are concerned that you are playing the "buttinsky" in something that is the parents' business, ask them. Chances are they will welcome all the help they can get in raising financially fit kids.

Letting Go

This is the time to kick your money mentoring team into high gear as one way to help kids move beyond the safety of the family realm and into the sphere of the larger world.

In this stage, some of the work may be harder for the family than for the young apprentice. Letting go is not always an easy task for family members. If the teen is eager and ready to break away, the family may feel ambivalent about this young independent in their midst. Knowing that the very act of giving your children skills for independence may well mean they will truly need you less can feel like a wrenching loss. On the other hand, if the child is wary of the world and seems to be avoiding independence, the family urge to protect may be at odds with the knowledge that life is not a rehearsal and that helping your child weave her own financial safety net is the most loving thing you can do.

The most common lament heard from parents at Independent Means (especially among mothers) is this: "I wish someone had talked with me about money when I was young." For many adults there is also the sadness and regret that comes with knowing that early financial competency might have made very different life choices available to them and their families.

Taking liberty with one of Robert Frost's great poems, we know that families are a place where, when you have to go there, they have to take you in. In a deep way, families are the most basic safety nets, and for many kids, this can be tough to give up. And for parents in today's "sandwich generation"— facing the dual pressures of educating kids and caring for aging parents—it's especially imperative to help kids become self-reliant so there are sufficient resources available for the *whole* family.

These conflicting realities—the profound awareness that we live in a world that requires financial competency at an early age, and the desire to keep kids close—mean that the work of the final stage of apprenticeship may be as much the emotional work of parents as the skill-building and risk-taking efforts of their kids. Acknowledging this in some explicit way will make a significant difference in how the last stage of your teen's financial apprenticeship plays out.

I f you can steer the arguments into conversations about what your teen wants his choices to add up to in his life, increasingly you will be able to leave the big decisions to him, trusting that he will make the right ones.

Rite of Passage: Independence Dinner

When your child is 16 or 17, it may be helpful to have a family night out to discuss self-reliance and independence. Dressing up, going to a grown-up restaurant, encouraging a positive and lively atmosphere for the evening, and making it clear that this is a night to talk about him will go a long way toward getting your child's attention. Own your role in the process of helping him become independent. Let him know that you love him, that watching him grow up is one of the most exciting elements of your life. Then ask him how he feels about his emerging desire for independence. Ask him to talk about his fears and dreams about what independence means. Then share your own fears and hopes.

The goal of this dinner is to mark a passage, to let your teenager know that you are aware of the changes that are now starting, that you have your own concerns, but that you also understand that together you need to figure out a path to independence and self-reliance that is as respectful and loving as you can make it.

Launching a conversation about shifting from dependence on family to increasing self-reliance puts a topic on the table that you will be able to revisit, discuss, think about, and experiment with. When tensions emerge because your child wants to go too fast (or slow) and you want her to slow down (or speed up) in that process, you now have a basis for talking together. You can now say, "Remember the night we went to dinner and discussed how we each might have a different tolerance level for how fast or how slow this process is unfolding?" Or, "Remember how we discussed the ways we will each trigger the other's fears or anxieties about the process? It looks like that may be hap-pening now. Let's talk about our feelings about dependence and self-reliance instead of yelling at each other about a specific event."

Whenever possible, move the conflict to the next-higher level of discourse. When you are arguing about whether or not your daughter can go on an expensive ski trip with friends or airing your frustration that it is only the middle of the month and your son has already spent his allowance, it's important to remember that these conflicts may not be primarily about the money! You are really arguing about matters of discipline, judgment, and values. If you can steer the arguments into conversations about what your teen wants his choices to add up to in his life, increasingly you will be able to leave the big decisions to him, trusting that he will make the right ones.

The Financial Expedition

Completing the financial apprenticeship is a rite of passage, much like taking a driver's test or voting for the first time. Below you will find six Financial Expeditions to help move your financial apprentice into full engagement with the world beyond the family. Think of these as Apprenticeship Final Exams—tasks that allow your kids to demonstrate to you and to themselves that they have mastered the Ten Basic Money Skills and are truly ready to be on their own.

With your teen, select one or more of the following projects to be completed by the last year of the apprenticeship (ideally age 18, but this may vary with your kids). Ask for a plan and a timeline for how she will execute the project—then hold her to it. Don't spring this task on kids as a surprise; best to lay the groundwork earlier.

Demonstrating resourcefulness. Problem solving is the goal of this challenge. Give your teen a choice of tasks to be accomplished:

- Make dinner for six (invite friends if you need to) on $30—and no, a take-out dinner doesn't count.
- For each family member, create birthday gifts on which he spends less than $5 each. The challenge here is to use creativity to dazzle the recipient, not just come up with low-cost solutions!
- Take a group of friends to a movie, a museum, a concert, or some other event

without paying for her ticket (sneaking into the theater is not an option). This may require developing a deal with the theater or museum to get one free ticket in return for guaranteeing a certain minimum number of attendees. Or it may include offering a special service that allows your teen to charge a bit extra for each ticket, covering her own entry fee: a lecture about the place the kids are visiting, or a ride in a limo to get there, for instance.

- Get an interview for his "dream" summer job or internship.

Making a journey. Decide on a destination with your teen and ask him to plan a trip there. It can be a real trip the family will take in the near future or a dream vacation. Make sure the plan includes a budget, transportation details, an itinerary, and a list of needed resources.

Selecting an investment. Allocate $100 for the purchase of stock. Have your teen select and research a stock, then select a company or website through which she can purchase stock. (Depending on her age, you may need to execute the final purchase, but everything up to that point should be in her care.) Ask her to track this stock over time and let you know how it's doing.

Making a philanthropic contribution. Allocate at least $100 (preferably from your teen's savings) to make a donation to a local charity or cause. Ask for a report on the organization's cause, documentation of interviews with the group being donated to, and a plan for how to track the impact of the donation over time.

Making a difference. Ask your teen to design and complete a project that makes a positive contribution to the community. It could be raising money for a particular cause or political campaign or organizing a group to offer community education on an issue that has gotten little attention. Make sure your teen specifies: (1) the purpose of the project; (2) an organizational plan; (3) the resources he will need and how he will acquire them; and (4) the intended outcomes. Stress that he doesn't have to change the whole world (though he might); the purpose of the challenge is to be aware of what goes into making a commitment to make a difference. If you think his project may be bigger in scale than he can successfully accomplish, back off and let him discover that himself—this is a learning project, not a no-fail project.

Executing a business venture. Challenge your teen to make a sum of money with a business venture. Whether it's organizing a car wash, setting up a babysitting service, or selling a product, the critical part of this project is to create a business plan and make a profit.

Moving On

If you and your kids have gotten this far in the Apprenticeship journey, you've probably succeeded in providing a solid financial foundation for your kids. Remembering that the journey has been not just about the money but also about launching great kids, you may ask yourself:

- Is my teen self-sufficient?
- Is my teen aware of what he/she is spending and how?
- Is my teen saving regularly?
- Do I trust my teen to be financially responsible? Do I respect his or her growing independence?
- Does my family share a set of financial values and do we walk our talk?
- Does my teen demonstrate integrity and good character in handling her or his financial life?
- In a life crisis (job loss, ill spouse, or divorce), will my teen have the financial acumen to cope with changed circumstances?

Kids who can and do learn how to pursue their dreams while managing the realities of money, and who are generous of heart with what they earn, become remarkable individuals. They are also safer in the world than their peers who are financially oblivious. Raising financially fit kids is a challenging undertaking for all parents, but the results will last a lifetime—and beyond, as your kids teach their own kids sound financial values.

Part Three

Side Trips

" I think the girl
who is able to earn her
own living and pay
her own way should be
as happy as anybody
on earth."

SUSAN B. ANTHONY

Money and Gender

When it comes to money, gender matters.

Neither Cinderella nor Snow White ever went out on a white horse in search of a special boy to carry off to a shining castle, there to live happily ever after on her fortune.

Fair or not, from Mexico to Morocco, Miami to Minneapolis, there is still an ingrained assumption that little boys will be breadwinners and little girls will have *a choice* about being breadwinners. Our history, our fairy tales and literature, and our assumptions guide how we integrate kids into the economic web of the community. Boys frequently have the benefit of an informal (if not very thoughtful) apprenticeship; girls often miss it altogether.

The result is that women tend to spend ages 21 to 35+ playing economic catch-up: falling into and getting out of debt; starting investments and businesses later than their male peers; and undercharging for their time, talents, and products. Sometimes they marry or get involved with men for economic reasons, pragmatically assessing that a man is one answer to the question: how will I take care of myself? For boys and men, the net effect may be a narrowed sense of options, with the burden of breadwinning on their shoulders. According to the most recent U.S. Census data, only about 12 percent of U.S. households are headed by women.

> I do think that parents who are conscious of history will help both their sons and daughters explore ways to integrate their life values with their economic values.

Gloria Steinem, defending Take Our Daughters to Work Day some years ago—when the only question that seemed to get any press was "what about the boys?"—said that "boys need a Take Our Sons Home Day." She was trying to make the very apt point that our tendency to peg our sons and daughters into specific economic and social roles has consequences that narrows life for both of them—and that if we want them to be financially secure with a full range of life options, we have to give them each a window on the world they see too little of: for girls, the world of commerce; for boys, the world of nurturing home life.

Gender Assumptions

As you select activities from the Life/Money Maps, keep in mind that financial literacy is not a genderless pursuit; it is packaged in centuries of tradition and assumptions. For example:

Boys trade, girls collect. The nature of children's play affects their adult competencies. Boys start to trade and barter as soon as they have something to exchange—maybe it's marbles, then *Pokemon* or *Yu-Gi-Oh!*, then it's *Magic: The Gathering* cards or baseball trading cards, then collectible coins or stamps.

In this way kids learn how to trade, almost unconsciously acquiring the language and the skills to assess value, negotiate, and keep track of their transactions.

"I just always knew," the 10-year-old son of a friend told me (with a profound air of condescension) when I asked how he had learned to trade. At the time he was in the midst of a high-level deal to sell a basketball card for $20 for which he had originally paid $3. His 12-year-old brother, meanwhile, was trying to sell a $300 card. This was high finance disguised as a game. No wonder venture capitalists complain that men routinely create business plans for the Billion-Dollar Business while women are still presenting plans for the Ten-Million-Dollar Deal. Boys simply have more practice visualizing extra zeros in their deals at an earlier age. By the time boys are old enough to buy and sell stocks, it is simply the next game—no big deal.

Meanwhile, the boys' sisters are collecting. Those Barbies and Beanie Babies are cute—and maybe the girls have put a few away that never came out of the box and may be worth something someday—but the skills of transaction are not being acquired. Being careful means that a girl will not get the great benefit and learning associated with making mistakes until she is much older, delaying her transition from financial novice to DollarDiva by years that can best be counted by the compound interest not accruing.

Girls babysit and are nurturing, good with kids; boys mow lawns and are enterprising, good with money. Try this next time you are with a group of adults or kids. Ask the question: how many of you had businesses when you were little kids? If it's a coed group, chances are most of the men and only a few women will raise their hands. If it's a women's-only or girls-only group, the same thing will happen: only a few hands will go up. Now, ask: how many of you babysat for money when you were kids? Immediately, about 90 percent of the female hands will go up.

When girls babysit it is often framed as something they do to help out because they are inherently good with kids (whether or not that's true). Boys may also make good babysitters, but they are usually called only *after* the local pool of girls has been tapped out. Meanwhile, when Danny comes home and announces he has four lawns lined up to mow over the weekend, it's unlikely he'll hear "Aren't you good with lawns!" Rather, he'll be praised for being resourceful, enterprising, and ambitious. He will start to see himself as others see him—a young and promising entrepreneur, not a lawn nurturer (which he may also be).

The messages we reflect back to our kids are part of how they discover their identities. As we help kids think of themselves as financial beings, they will begin to act accordingly. The next time your daughter comes to you with an idea for a business or a question about money—no matter how naïve the query—resist any urge to call her behavior or plans "cute." Remember that she is practicing the concepts and language of money that will help her become a self-confident and self-reliant adult.

Boys are raised to make money; girls to do good. Since the 1980s there has been a small but persistent movement in business to create and nurture more socially responsible businesses. The Body Shop, Ben & Jerry's, Burt's Bees, Stonybrook Yogurt, Timberland, and Tom's of Maine are examples of companies that have tried, often with great success, to transcend the bifurcation of business and philanthropy. Emerging out of the consciousness of the '70s, the socially responsible business movement gave both men and women new options for combining their quest to make a living with the quest for a meaningful life. But it is still a nascent model, and often under siege in a world in which dog-eat-dog values trump win-win solutions, competition outweighs cooperation, and having it all seems more important than sharing some.

Historically, women—especially relatively privileged white women—were steered into the "do good" side of life that included education, nonprofits, and health care, while men were steered into making money. The vestiges of all the old models are still with us, and until we reach a state in which both men and women share equal opportunities for pursuing their life goals, the gender difference will continue to have some bearing on relative income and earning potential.

I don't think that shifting girls away from values related to doing good is the answer to greater financial equality. But I do think that parents who are conscious of history will help both their sons and daughters explore ways to integrate their life values with their economic values.

Men are paid for most of the work they do; women are not. Women are penalized by government policy. Every paid worker may qualify for social security, unemployment insurance, or worker's compensation, but mothers do not. Nannies earn social security, but mothers do not. Motherhood is the single greatest risk factor for poverty in old age.

Money and Gender: The Numbers

Obviously these observations are not operative in all families. If you are one of the contemporary families that have transcended gender, feel free to skip this chapter—your daughter may be the next CEO of a Fortune 500 company and your son may discover that his home based-business will give him greater opportunity to experience his kids. It happens. But before you skip ahead, consider these numbers:

- Ninety percent of all girls will have to take care of themselves economically at some point in their lives.
- One in three women workers earns less than $20,000 per year; in contrast, only one in five men earns less than $20,000.
- Sixteen percent of men work who full-time earn at least $75,000 per year; only 6 percent of women working full-time make that much.
- The average total compensation of the thirty highest-paid male executives in the U.S. is $112.9 million. The average total compensation of the thirty highest-paid female executives is only $8.9 million.
- In 2000, women held only 6 percent of the highest-ranking leadership positions and 12 percent of corporate officer positions. Women of color represented only 1 percent of corporate officers.
- When asked to list future career choices, girls aged 9 to 14 selected business careers only 9 percent of the time; boys listed them 15 percent of the time.
- Eighty-five percent of the elderly poor are women.
- The average woman's standard of living falls by 45 percent the first year after a divorce and 37 percent thereafter; the average man sees a 15 percent improvement.
- One in seven women does not have a retirement account; one in three women with both a retirement account and credit cards owes more on credit cards than she has in her retirement account.

Economic Self-Defense for Girls: A First-Aid Kit

Applying the Ten Basic Money Skills will give your daughter the tools she needs to take care of herself—no matter what happens to you, or what occurs in her marriage, her job, her investments, the economy, or the sociopolitical environment. If you are growing concerned that your daughter's money style can best be described as that of the spendthrift or the oblivious and you want to intervene in more forceful ways, here are some additional tactics you can employ.

Give your daughter well-written woman-oriented books for birthdays, for good grades, or for no reason at all.

By the time she is 13 or 14 she is ready for books like *Prince Charming Isn't Coming: How Women Get Smart About Money* by Barbara Stanny or, for younger girls, *New Moon Money: How to Get It, Spend It, and Save It*. Let her know that you take her seriously and feel she is ready to be responsible about her economic future. When she turns 15 or 16, give her a subscription to *Business Week* or *Fortune*—she may think you a little strange, but she will tell all her friends about it!

Start a mother-daughter investment club

Enlist her friends and their mothers to tackle money issues together and have a good time. The best investment clubs are started to help girls and women become educated about money and how to manage it: make sure you are with a group of learners who will provide a supportive environment for the group. This can work with girls as young as 12 or 13. Combining the club meetings with other experiences (dinner together, a movie after the meeting) will also give the experience a more appealing edge. For guidance on starting an investment club, see page 114–115.

Immerse your daughter in a sea of positive female role models

She may not want to hear your lecture on why she needs to be financially prepared (the future can seem so far away to an adolescent or teen), but she may listen to stories from other women. This may be the time to create a new money mentoring team—one composed entirely of women. Line them up for a month of after-school events or Saturday morning visits. The intensity of the sessions may be enough to get your daughter's attention—and if she has chemistry with at least one of the women, something will stick. Stories shared by women who have bought a first house, sold a business, or acquired a job she loves (even if it doesn't come with a giant salary) can be powerful examples for a young woman trying to grasp her own identity.

One of Independent Means's most popular DollarDiva Workshops includes an activity called Rotating Interviews. In it, more than fifty girls are introduced to ten or more female role models. The girls are organized in small groups and given fifteen minutes to interview one of the role models. They can ask anything they want about her personal/economic/social life (the role models can choose not to answer a question if it becomes too personal, of course!). At the end of fifteen minutes, the girls rotate to interview one of the other role models in the room. By the time an hour has passed, the girls have all gotten some exposure to at least four role models. This may not seem to be a lot of time, but remember that these are kids who multitask at the computer while doing their homework—they can extract a lot of information in fifteen minutes, especially when acting as a group.

At the end of the interviews, the girls reconvene as a large group and are asked to share what they thought the women had in common and what about them was unique. Invariably, one of the observations the girls make—regardless of family background, ethnic identity, or economic status—is that "few of the women are doing today what they thought they would be doing when they were our age."

This revelation—that you do not have to, and indeed *cannot* have all the answers to your life, but that you will still be successful—seems to provide enormous relief to these girls. They gain permission to explore and make mistakes, to see themselves as having something in common with these clearly interesting, financially independent women. Being able to identify with successful women is a heap more palatable for many girls than following Mom's advice.

The Macroeconomics of Girls and Money

By applying the strategies and activities offered above and in the preceding chapters, you can be fairly confident you are raising a financially fit daughter. But what about the big picture: the macroeconomics of the world she and her friends are entering?

- Research tells us that 95 percent of top-earning corporate officers are still male. *Does it make you uneasy to think that when your 12-year-old daughter is 29, she may be battling a glass ceiling?*
- 46 percent of all privately held businesses are owned by women, but women have access to only 2.3 percent of the available capital to fund those businesses. *What if your daughter wants to start a business? How will she get the capital to fund it?*
- During the same week in the spring of 2003 that the Bush administration launched a massive attack on Title IX (which was later dropped as a result of mass public resistance and parental activism)—the legislation passed in 1972 to help equalize the support for and participation of girls in sports— the New York Times published a cover story on the increasing arms race among colleges to pay $1-million-plus salaries for football coaches. *In this context, are you concerned that your daughter and her friends don't have adequate showers in their locker room while boys are still getting a whopping $133 million more in athletic scholarships each year than are girls?*

Making sure your daughter has the financial skills and knowledge to take care of herself is important. But the world beyond her is worthy of attention too. The difficulty in widening this perspective came home to me personally some years ago when, while writing my first book, I created an "Agenda for Girls." Devising a wish list for improving the future of girls, I listed a number of issues, policies, and programs I felt were important. And then it occurred to me to call for a substantial investment in girls. This was 1989, before Take Our Daughters to Work Day, before the movement for girls' self-esteem and economic empowerment had really begun. So as I sat at my computer I tried to come up with a dollar amount that would suit my dream.

My first thought was a meager $1 million. It only took a minute before I dismissed that number as trivial in the face of a U.S. population of twenty-six million girls. So I moved on to $10 million, and dismissed that number as well after I realized that a single fighter jet cost more—and girls were certainly worth a few jets. By now I was on a roll. A $100 million investment in girls—what might that do for their future? Now I was getting excited, so I pressed on. A billion dollars, I thought—why not a *$1 billion* investment in the future of girls?

And then, as though an electric current shot through my body, my hands jumped off my keyboard and I thought: *people will laugh at me if I write that down.* And then I realized: *that's the problem.* If I, a committed advocate for girls, couldn't comfortably call for making a billion-dollar investment in the future of girls, who could? Who would?

The economic well-being of girls depends on a complex interaction of policy decisions, financial investments, educational commitments, and personal action. Raised ourselves not to take girls seriously, not to see them as warranting the same kind of investment the other natural resources of this country receive, we find it hard to change old habits. How can we show our commitment to supporting our daughters, granddaughters, nieces, foster children, and all their daughters to come?

Gender and Money: Activism for Daughters

Among the new voices that lobby for girls today, two groups stand out: New Moon Publishing (www.newmoon.org) and its partner organization, Dads and Daughters (www.dadsanddaughters.org). New Moon, started in 1993 by Nancy Gruver, was among the first organizations to listen to and talk directly with girls about their hopes and dreams; later they began to share with parents what they were learning from their daughters. In the last few years, after purchasing the distinguished *Daughters' Newsletter for Parents of Girls*, they have become one of the most potent groups advocating passionately on behalf of girls. Gruver's husband, Joe Kelly, father of two daughters, launched Dads and Daughters (DAD) in 1999 to draw fathers into a new activism on behalf of girls. Over the last few years, the two organizations have taken on a couple of big sacred cows, mobilizing parents to act on behalf of their daughters. Among their efforts:

Campaigns to stop the sexual exploitation of girls in ads

One of the most egregious campaigns to get the attention of DAD was an ad placed by Macy's for Buffalo Jeans in the August 2002 issue of *CosmoGirl* magazine. DAD immediately attacked the ad—which showed a girl sexily posed with her pants pulled down and her hand placed in perfect masturbation mode—and brought it to the attention of the massive DAD network of members and supporters. Though Macy's did not respond to the initial cry of outrage, DAD continued to press the issue and finally engaged the company in a dialogue about best practices. Parents *can* affect the way companies treat their kids. This is just one example of how parental attentiveness to the connections between money and gender can make a difference for children.

How does this relate to the financial well-being of daughters? Remember that one of the Ten Basic Money Skills is to spend wisely, which includes being a savvy consumer. This means that girls need to be aware of how their money (and yours) is being targeted, and by whom. Teaching them to vote with their wallets is a way of giving them power and a voice. Letting advertisers know you are paying attention to the messages they send to your daughters, holding their feet to the fire when necessary, is a way of making clear that you, too, will vote with your wallet.

Advocacy for Title IX

Thirty years after the passage of this legislation, which prohibited sex discrimination in federally assisted education programs, 55 percent of post–Title IX–generation girls participated in high school sports, compared to 36 percent of pre–Title IX–generation girls. And numerous studies have now demonstrated the profound effect of that legislation on everything from higher test scores in school to lower pregnancy rates. The very existence of the WNBA and professional women's soccer is a tribute to the long-term effects of the law.

Still, thirty years later, recruiting budgets for female athletes are only 32 percent of total recruiting budgets. In the majority of high school athletic programs nationwide, girls still struggle for equity in equipment, facilities, scheduling of games, and practice times. Nevertheless, at the end of 2002, the Commission on Opportunity in Athletics, appointed by the U.S. Department of Education, was ready to recommend the removal of the law's equality standards, allowing institutions to treat female athletes like second-class citizens, dramatically reducing their opportunities to participate and receive scholarship dollars.

DAD (along with most other girl-serving organizations) went into high gear to notify its membership that it was time to send letters to decision makers to help prevent this financial crime against girls. A national educational campaign, Save Title IX (www.savetitleix.org), was launched by the National Coalition for Women and Girls in Education, mobilizing grassroots organizations, elected public officials, athletes, and celebrities to address this issue. In July 2003, the administration announced that it had backed off its efforts to dismantle the legislation.

Advocacy for Title IX is not one of the Ten Basic Money Skills. But awareness of who supports the dismantling of a program that benefits girls so profoundly is one facet of a larger understanding of the gender politics affecting your daughters. These two examples are a small slice of the actions that can and must be taken on behalf of girls if we wish to avoid the need for remedial work with women's financial empowerment generation after generation. There's a lot of work to be done. Pick your own battle for girls' economic well-being and make a difference!

Boys, Money, and Gender

If gender has such an impact on girls' economic well-being, what is the impact on boys? It's different, but certainly not insignificant. Among the issues that may be elephants lurking about in your son's bedroom are:

> **Gender Challenges for Boys**
> Role assumptions
> Shame
> Values
> Prowess

Role assumptions

"There are choices I have to make—career, income expectations—because I'm the guy." Asked by the U.S. Embassy in Mexico City to run a workshop for teens there, I found myself in a room with one hundred middle-class Mexican teens, both boys and girls. Launching into the Ten Basic Money Skills, I came to the section of the workshop where I deal with money talk. Engaging the kids in their own learning, I decided to have them role-play a discussion of a date and who would pay for what.

One young man had the temerity to ask, "Why should I pay for this date? I don't have any more money than she does." Pandemonium broke out!

Challenging the most ingrained of assumptions in his culture, speaking his mind on a taboo topic, this brave young man incurred the wrath of many of the girls in the room while his pals looked on with awe. For the next twenty minutes emotions soared as boys finally had a chance to say, "Coming up with the cash to take a girl out regularly is hard." Meanwhile, the girls, fearful of giving up a tradition—and a privilege—fought to make a case for why the boys should continue to buy into this ancient assumption.

In Mexico City as in Minneapolis, boys are questioning societal assumptions—just as girls and women have been doing for a long time now. But without support and a forum for their queries—a broader discussion among adults who care about boys and take them seriously—boys will be continue to be restless, uncertain, confused, and angry about how to deal with cultural expectations.

In a series of workshops in the U.S. in the spring of 2003, I interviewed more than three hundred high school girls, representing a broad mix of race and class. Fully one-third of those girls described "boyfriends" as part of their financial plan. This disjunction between boys' readiness for less burdensome financial relationships and girls' expectations of the traditional role for boys will be a big part of the dialogue between the sexes in the next decade.

For young men, role assumptions have direct financial consequences. Whether trapping them in the role of breadwinner, equating their worth with the size of their paycheck, or imposing pressure to keep up with friends' tech toys and wheels, money has the power to tell young men who they are—or are not—in an insidious way. Parents who give their boys a chance to express their concerns and worries about the economic assumptions of their lives offer these young men alternatives to culturally imposed pressures as they grow into independent adults.

Shame

"Boys are supposed to know these things. I'm too embarrassed to ask for help." We joke about men who won't ask for directions when they get lost, but when money equals a man's worth, how much more shameful and difficult it is for a boy to admit he has no idea what a balance sheet is, can't tell a CD from a DVD, has no idea how to negotiate the purchase of a car, and can't compute compound interest any more than he can recite *The Odyssey* backwards (or forwards!).

Young men who seem to reject parental advice about money, who act out, spend recklessly, or otherwise challenge their parents on economic issues may in fact be using bravado and rebellion to cover their lack of competency. Help them master the Ten Basic Money Skills and see how their anxiety, shame, and anger is defused as they complete their financial apprenticeship.

Values

The complex dilemmas that boys grapple with often have an economic component. Boys are vulnerable to media images, the unconscious desires of parents, and the pressure of peers for whom gender roles may be exaggerated in the adolescent and teen years. Consider these statements made by boys at Independent Means programs:

- I'd like to become a forest ranger (or an artist, or start a nonprofit) but unless I make a lot of money, I know my parents will be disappointed in me.
- At my house, both my parents work. But when I get married, I want my wife to stay home.
- I know I'm supposed to follow in my father's footsteps and become a lawyer, but frankly, what I really want to do is get an internship with a top chef and open my own restaurant someday.

▪ I'm dating a girl who I think has a big trust fund. She always has more spending money than I do and I can't take her to the kinds of places she is used to going on her dates. I don't want to lose her but don't know how to talk with her about the differences in our lives.

As a parent, grandparent, or money mentor, how can you help young men address and resolve these life-defining dilemmas? Like so many things I discuss in this book, often the simplest solutions are the most useful. In this case, talking about the issues and making sure boys meet role models who have already grappled (successfully and not) with the same issues is probably the most help you can offer.

The loneliness and isolation of boys who think they're the only ones to feel this way is a big source of depression. Drawing boys into relationships that let them articulate and deal with their worst-case fears doesn't take great psychological skill—only compassion and acceptance.

Prowess

In a world in which cool rules and the one with the most toys wins, boys who do not have a strong materialist bent, who do not feel deeply about the need to show off the latest digital products, may feel self-conscious about their lack of interest in the behavior of "real boys." One aspect of the financial apprenticeship for boys is claiming a sense of who they are, apart from the benchmarks for success that they think they are supposed to exhibit. Letting your son know that his self-worth is not just about net worth is a key part of the message you can pass along.

Making Change: Tactics for Parents

Make yourself knowledgeable (and vocal) about school policies related to gender equity and economic development for kids.

Let your local and national politicians know that if they expect your vote, they need to pass muster on issues related to the financial well-being of your children.

When you see an ad or product that exploits girls (or boys), take a moment to send the company an email or letter that cries foul (or send an email to Dads and Daughters and they may share the concern with their members).

Write an op-ed piece for a local paper about how to involve girls in the economic life of the community and give boys more options in the community's social life.

Talk about money and gender at the dinner table.

Keep an eye on your former college: has the male/female ratio of professors changed dramatically since you graduated? If not, withhold your annual contribution and write a letter to the head of development explaining why you're doing so.

Gender and Economics

Without embroiling your kids in gender wars before they can spell *gender*, you can support and equip your sons and daughters to live in a century in which responsibilities are shared, roles are blurred, and options—social and economic—are both more diverse and more complex. Without the comforting (if constricting) structure of rigid roles and social obligations, kids will have to make up their own rules and sort out their own responsibilities. Mastery of the Ten Basic Money Skills is as liberating for boys as for girls. And kids with a grounding in financial literacy will be able to construct a new world by choice—not by default.

" To fulfill a dream,
to be allowed to
sweat over lonely labor,
to be given a chance to
create, is the meat
and potatoes of life.
The money is the gravy. "

BETTE DAVIS

Raising Rich Kids

One night I had just finished giving a talk to a group of parents in a reasonably affluent community. A few people stayed behind to ask questions and chat, but one father waited patiently off to the side. When everyone else had left, he approached me with his dilemma. "My son is 19. He has a BMW, his own gas card, another credit card. He lives at home and doesn't pay rent; he wants for nothing. But I am now afraid he doesn't have the strengths he needs to live independently and pursue goals of his own. I've been putting off the 'big money talk' for too long and am determined to address it now. Can you tell me where to start?"

My heart went out to this loving father who had given his son everything except a financial apprenticeship and now wanted to find a quick way to make up for the oversight. How to begin?

Resources for Raising Affluent Kids

Spoiling Childhood: How Well-Meaning Parents Are Giving Children Too Much—But Not What They Need, Diane Ehrensaft

I've Known Rivers: Lives of Loss and Liberation, Sarah Lawrence-Lightfoot

Silver Spoon Kids: How Successful Parents Raise Responsible Children, Eileen Gallo and Jon Gallo

Wealth in Families, Charles Collier

More than Money journal, www.morethanmoney.org

Family Office Exchange (FOX), independent advisor to families of exceptional wealth: www.foxexchange.com

Resource Generation, www.resourcegeneration.org (617) 225-3939

Family Firm Institute, www.ffi.org

It's Not Just About the Money

I often meet and work with family foundations and organizations serving affluent families—and over and over we arrive at a point of view that underscores the ideas in this book. When it comes to kids and money, it's *not* just about the money.

What these families struggle with is how to raise great kids with positive values, good hearts, a measure of discipline, and a life of purpose and meaning. When a child is, at birth or shortly thereafter, "set for life," how does a parent help the child develop aspirations to achieve and an awareness of privilege as a responsibility, not an entitlement. How do parents and grandparents help children learn that abundance of spirit may be more important than abundance of material goods? How does a child who has only known private jets and multiple homes develop empathy with the inequities of social organization? And how do parents who have themselves inherited their fortune pass along a respect for family legacy as well as a vision of the future that guides the growth and shepherding of family assets?

How, in other words, do you give kids with everything the guidance to manage more?

Guidelines for Raising Kids amidst Affluence

Often affluent parents will say to me, "We're fortunate that our kids don't have to worry about money." My heart sinks for those children.

While no kid should have to *worry* about money, you want your child to be cognizant and conscious of his or her privileges and responsibilities regarding money. Kids raised in a never-never land of financial freedom often grow up in a state of suspended reality. These kids are more likely to struggle with identity issues, lack of confidence, and questions of worth and spirituality, and may display a significant lack of concern for or awareness of others.

Indeed, Jessie H. O'Neill, author of *The Golden Ghetto: The Psychology of Affluence,* warns that children of affluence are prone to:

- Inability to delay gratification
- Inability to tolerate frustration
- Low self-esteem and self-worth
- Lack of self-confidence
- False sense of entitlement
- Loss of future motivation

O'Neill ascribes these dysfunctions to material satiation and emotional deprivation. While there is insufficient evidence that wealthy kids experience emotional deprivation in any greater incidence than kids from any other income group, it is clear that children who "have it all" often do experience missing "something." That something may be the intangible, internal sense of a world in which they can make a difference, experience meaningful connections with others, and feel a sense of purpose.

A number of books have been written about the dark side of affluence. Among them are *Privileged Ones: The Well-Off and Rich in America* (volume five of the *Children of Crisis* series) by Pulitzer Prize–winning child psychiatrist Robert Coles and, more recently, Lee Hausner's book *Children of Paradise: Successful Parenting for Prosperous Families.* Both books examine the disadvantages of having it all and are useful references for families experiencing developmental crises with affluent children.

However, my intent here is not to focus on the dark side of wealth (or the crushing problems inherent in having nothing, for that matter), but to help you raise great kids with sound values amidst great wealth.

For children of wealth, the Ten Basic Money Skills offer tools and a structure for understanding their wealth and managing it in ways that are connected to a deeper meaning than having the most toys, living the most "worry-free" life, or accruing the most exotic experiences.

Whether your kids will one day be expected to run a family business, start businesses of their own, oversee the family philanthropies, or simply manage their own incomes, they will need to understand the language of money, the questions they need to ask of advisors, and the criteria for distinguishing good advice from bad. Young people who are "protected" from financial knowledge and skills are left most vulnerable right at the moment they need to make significant financial decisions about their assets.

For children of wealth, the Ten Basic Money Skills offer tools and a structure for understanding their wealth and managing it in ways that are connected to a deeper meaning than having the most toys, living the most "worry-free" life, or accruing the most exotic experiences.

Fill the Void: Talk

Don't put it off until you can "say the right thing." Saying things awkwardly is better than not saying anything at all. While talking with your kids about money is important, whatever the family financial status, the need is exponentially increased when vast resources are available. It's a mistake to think that because kids do not ask questions directly about the family assets, they aren't thinking about them. Kids have active imaginations and will fill the void with their fantasies if reality isn't available to them.

Perhaps your kids vastly overestimate the affluence of the family and assume they will never have to think about money, or perhaps they worry about what-ifs: what if something happens to Mom or Dad? If Mom and Dad don't leave for the office every day, how do they make money? What does it mean that their lives are dramatically different from their friends'? It's also important to preempt information your kids may get inadvertently from other family members, friends, parents of friends, or neighbors. When kids pick up innuendos, fragments of information, or misinformation, they may be more confused than ever.

Parents who convince themselves that their children aren't aware of their wealth or don't need to know the facts kid themselves about just how intuitive and sensitive children are. Kids generally know much more, much sooner about many things than parents are willing to acknowledge. In many cases the issue is not what the child is *ready to hear* now but what the parent is comfortable *sharing* now. If this is the case in your family, call on your kids' money mentoring team for help. Or talk with other parents in similar circumstances about how they handle money talk in their families. Avoiding the subject because no one helped you to talk about money comfortably when you were a kid does the next generation a distinct disservice. Helping kids integrate and make sense of money as it relates to family will go a long way toward building their trust in you, as well as their own confidence that there are no family secrets.

While their values may ultimately diverge from yours as they mature, your kids need to hear what you believe in and why you believe it. One aunt related to me the experience of being with her niece on a shopping expedition. The 12-year-old wanted her aunt to purchase an outfit the aunt felt was inappropriate for her niece's age. The aunt was also concerned that the manufacturer was not one she wanted to patronize.

"I could well afford to buy the outfit," the woman told me later. "But I had a 'teachable moment' and decided to grab it. I explained to her that I had concerns about the exploitation of girls and women and that I had seen an ad for that brand in a fashion magazine that left me feeling uneasy about the way women were portrayed by that company. She wasn't happy with me, but she listened. And she could see that I didn't buy things just because I can; that I make conscious decisions about what I buy and why."

Money talk strikes at the heart of issues of self-worth, visions of the world, and values about relationships among loved ones and friends. If kids cannot develop a comfort level with this conversation at home, it will be harder for them to develop it outside the home in other relationships, both business and personal. Money talk tells your kids you respect them, love them, and care about their ability to communicate with others.

Model Your Money Values

"I'm an early adopter," one dad told me. "I have every new tech toy that comes out. The latest PDA, telecom gadgets, music equipment, you name it. Part of that is geek fascination, but part of it is that I want to have leading-edge things—and I can well afford them. If I'm like that, how I am I going to help my kids ignore what their peers do and have? How am I going to help them be more than materialist consumers?" This was a dad with insight. Aware that his affluence—and material desires—bumped up against the imperative for his kids to develop what he considered responsible values, he struggled with how to shelter them from the very behavior he practiced.

Perhaps in no other sphere is the issue of integrity more critical than in the realm of what you *tell* your kids are good values and what you *exhibit* in your own life—that is, literally integrating behavior with spoken values. Of course, the best parents are tolerant of their own and others' human frailties—you will not *at all times* model the behavior you hope your kids will practice. But if you want your children to be thoughtful about how and where they spend, invest, and give away their money, you (and your money mentoring team) will need to present a strong role model for those values. If you *only* buy designer labels and take your children to the finest boutiques, you're teaching your kids that they do not have to practice financial decision making.

So how can this dad bridge the gap between his own consumer behavior and his hope that his kids practice moderation? He can start by examining whether he really does need every tech toy on the market as soon as it's released. He might say to his 12-year-old:

- "Jack, I was going to purchase a new DVD player for the upstairs family room, but the one we have works pretty well still and I think I'd like to give the money to a nonprofit instead. Will you help me decide to whom we should make a contribution and why?"

- "Jack, I'm able to purchase this new BMW because I've (worked hard/ invested well/been fortunate to inherit from our family). There will be many things you'll want to have too. And though we are fortunate to be able to give you many material things, a more important thing I want to give you is the drive and ability to handle money responsibly, make good choices between wants and needs, and share with others. So though we have the resources to purchase many things, as you grow up I'm going to ask you to contribute some portion of the money to buy the things you want. You can work for that money or save it from your allowance, but it is important to me that you understand that working for the things that matter to you is an essential adult value."

- "Jack, the new _____ is available online tomorrow. We can order it for a premium price today, or we can wait a few months and purchase it at (name the discount house). Though I really am anxious to have it, I think we should wait and see if we can get it at a better price. We can take the difference and donate it to your (Boy Scout Troop, camera club, favorite cause)."
- "Jack, the new _____ is now on sale, but the company selling it has not cleaned up its (employment practices, ecological awareness). I'd like to wait until it is available from a company whose values are closer to ours."

In these instances the father is letting his son know that having things isn't an entitlement; it comes with responsibilities and choices. The more conscious you are about your purchases of material goods, the more conscious your kids will be about their own financial choices. Consuming isn't inherently bad—just be sure to be mindful of its impact on your child's values.

Say NO

In the summer of 2002, Seth Mydans reported in the *New York Times* that Prince Jefri Bolkiah, 48-year-old brother of the Sultan of Brunei, had frittered away *$15 billion* of the country's assets in a mere fifteen years or so, and in so doing had plundered a significant part of the legacy of oil that the 330,000 citizens of the Southeast Asian sultanate counted on to ensure a high quality of life. The Prince's escapades offer a rather extreme cautionary tale for families that never learn to say no.

One of the most frequently asked questions I get from affluent parents is this: my kids know we can afford to give them anything they want, so telling them we can't afford something is ridiculous. Whether it's buying that expensive sports car, spending thousands on the designer gown for her sorority dance, or springing for a half-million-dollar bar mitzvah, parents who can give their kids everything often do. So if you can provide it all, why not? Later, when the kids are showing signs of an identity crisis, depression, or callous lack of awareness of the needs and concerns of others, parental indulgence may turn to anger or frustration with their kids—or worse, to disregard of their emotional or spiritual restlessness.

Because *you can* is not a good enough reason to indulge your children's every desire—indeed, *because you can* may be a clear signal that you *shouldn't.*

Here is one way to provide a frame of reference for your kids: even very poor families may be able to afford a wealth of candy bars. But just because they can keep a cache of thirty or forty candy bars in the cupboard doesn't mean that it's a good idea to give their kids all those candy bars at once. Indeed, this is a sure prescription for indigestion, bad teeth, and a sugar high. So if the parents are at all responsible, they will withhold the candy bars and mete them out over time, *in moderation*, hoping to teach their kids about discipline, judgment, and responsibility in the process.

Parents at all income levels have a responsibility to teach their kids how to manage in the face of abundance as well as scarcity. And even when excess is an option, insisting on moderation—that kids pay their share, work for things they want, share with others, and exhibit evidence of the Ten Basic Money Skills—may be one of the most effective means of instilling responsibility. Indeed, one of the great tensions that affluent parents struggle to manage is their hope that their kids will somehow, magically, acquire some middle-class values (work hard, manage money responsibly, strive for excellence, delay gratification, practice moderation)—or at least more Warren Buffet–like values!

There are many famously affluent families (the Rockefellers, Kennedys, and Buffets, for example) that serve as models for having instilled these values in their kids. But it didn't happen by accident. It happened because the family vision was one in which the children of wealth understood their obligations to others and to the future. In other words, *because you can* is not a good enough reason to indulge your children's every desire—indeed, *because you can* may be a clear signal that you *shouldn't.*

Say Yes to Big Ideas

One of my favorite stories comes from an affluent mother who had not grown up with wealth herself. She and her husband, a successful entrepreneur, had made their fortune with the sale of several high-tech companies. They now had significant wealth and a set of values that included giving back as an imperative of their purpose as humans.

Their 14-year-old daughter had been raised with these values. She attended a private school that was right for her learning needs but not necessarily one of the most richly endowed. The school had a first-rate theater program that she became very active in, but it did not have a first-rate performance center.

The couple's children each received a sum of money to give away every year. When the 14-year-old announced that she wanted to give the school a proper theater, her school principal was surprised, to say the least—but her parents were filled with pride. Though the cost of the theater represented a good deal more money than she had been allotted to give away, they decided that her goal and her impulse were coming from the right place and they helped her see the project through to completion. This was a pretty ambitious undertaking for a 14-year-old, but one that would make a difference not just in her life but also in the lives of students who would attend the school for many years to come. She now understands what is involved in making a big dream come to fruition—and has both the experience and sophistication to engage in complicated projects in the future.

Saying yes to big ideas is as important as saying no to overindulgence. Particularly if children will have access to and the opportunity to manage vast assets, getting practice dealing with large-scale decisions early on is important. Children who will need to step up to the plate to manage large inheritances or trust funds will be ill-served by only having practice with micro-level projects or small decisions. If your child will have access to large sums when he is 21, giving him a tiny allowance to manage during his financial apprenticeship will not prepare him for the shift in scale that will occur with great speed.

Do the Math

Too often, children with trust funds may live with the false security that they and future generations will be able to live comfortably on interest from the capital that earlier generations have created. Howard H. Stevenson, the Sarofim-Rock Professor of Business Administration at Harvard University's Graduate School of Business Administration, gives a particularly compelling presentation for families in which he lays bare the math of how easy it is for families to go from the proverbial shirtsleeves to shirtsleeves in three generations.

As Professor Stevenson puts it, families grow, needs grow, and desires grow, but the math doesn't change. Using a case study, he describes a family business (it could also be manageable assets) for which he assumes an average growth rate of 4 percent for eighteen years:

$15 million in capital (in year 0) provides *$360,000* in interest

$30 million in capital (in year 18) provides *$729,000* in interest

In year eighteen, assuming that their desires have been growing at just 2 percent per year, the parents may reasonably spend $514,168 of the $729,000. This leaves a little under $215,000 for the kids. Although the average number of children per woman in the U.S. was just 2.07 in 2002, if your family has three or four children, you can see how quickly the numbers divide down. And as *their* kids come into the family, and divorce and remarriage exercise even more constraints on the original income, one can see that "something's gotta give."

Professor Stevenson lays out the bald choices:

- The entire family's living standards must decline (this is what we mean nowadays by downsizing our financial needs)
- The parents' living standards must stay flat or decline so that their kids can still be subsidized
- The company or source of wealth has to grow faster
- A new source of entrepreneurial energy must be infused into the family system

The bottom line, he emphasizes, is that even a great business with brilliant management can't support a growing family forever! When Professor Stevenson talks about wealth planning, "training the next generation" is at the top of his list of priorities. And when the next generation understands the math of the family assets, they are in a much more realistic and helpful position to contribute to the transition and creation of wealth, one generation to the next, rather than becoming parasites who are dependent upon it.

Keep Kids Informed

Families try a lot of strategies to keep their kids financially grounded. A favorite is not telling them exactly how wealthy the family actually is. The problem with withholding information is that it communicates a lack of trust, takes away from kids the chance to act responsibly, and leaves a void for fantasy and imagination that won't necessarily be filled in the ways you'd hope.

To that end, I always encourage telling the truth and expecting kids to be accountable to that truth. By the time they're in the last stage of their financial apprenticeship, your children need to know the family's financial advisors, the family financial plans, and their place in those plans. And by now, of course, your kids should be actively involved in planning their own financial futures. This the time to make sure they leave the nest with the tools and knowledge they need to make the transition to true adulthood.

It's part of the American Dream to hope your kids will do better, be better, and have it better than you did. Instilling in your children an awareness of why shepherding growth is critical to the future will give them—and subsequent generations—the best chance at living out that dream.

Visionaries and Caretakers: Scale as a Factor in Child Development

Wealthy kids are as diverse as any other group of kids. Some will emerge as great leaders, others as great followers; some will be quirky and individualistic, others will join the crowd at every opportunity. Some will be brilliant, others not so. Kindness and evil will be as evenly dispersed as in any other group. Wealth brings no special immunity from the happenstance of genes or foibles of basic humanity, but it does bring opportunity and obligation on a different scale. And it is the factor of scale that parents must be prepared to deal with as their children grow up.

Children who grow up with limo drivers and private pilots, who assume their first car will be a BMW, and for whom a summer vacation means a skiing trip in the Andes, are not likely to be worrying about the pennies they drop into a piggy bank. Nevertheless, the Ten Basic Money Skills are still critical to their learning how they will manage their income from the family trusts, handle a monthly allowance that may be larger than the average family's income, and figure out who they are apart from the family assets.

How to handle scale is a challenge for the most thoughtful and sophisticated of families. Here are a few suggestions:

Frame Your Wealth

Do talk about what it means that the family has more resources than others. Give your kids some context. Introduce the family legacy—how was the wealth made? If it was handed down from earlier generations, make sure you convey the qualities and nature of the people who provided the gift. If affluence is a new state for the family and came from your own efforts, make sure you talk about your life before and after the assets were acquired. In other words, make sure you communicate that the wealth wasn't magic but emerged from the vision, ideas, risk-taking, and hard work of someone along the way. Talk about what the presence of wealth means for and demands of each family member.

Give Practice with Large Sums Early On

By the time kids are in their tweens (11, 12, 13), they can begin to practice with issues of scale. If a $10 per week allowance is reasonable for some kids in the context of family income but your child's allowance is more reasonably $100 per week, then give it to him—with some special demands. When dividing up where money from his allowance goes, require a substantially larger portion to be placed in savings and philanthropic accounts. Just because your child can spend more than his public school peers is not a good reason to give him ten times what his peers have, but giving him practice to think in larger and more ambitious ways about saving and contributing is appropriate and useful.

Involve Your Child in Big Decisions

Are you making a substantial investment in a new house or property for the family? Are you thinking of investing money in your business? Are you about to send a substantial payment to your child's private school or college? Talk with her about it. Obviously you will not take financial advice from a 10-year-old, and you won't choose a plot of land based on a 12-year-old's desires. But giving your children a voice in the family's large financial decisions sends the message that this is something they should know about and that they will one day have to make these kinds of decisions themselves.

Give Your Child a Voice with Your Family Investment Advisor

An advisor who can deal well (and not condescendingly) with your kids will be able to add an important educational service to their financial apprenticeship—and will also serve as another listening post for your kids. It may be that your adolescent is more comfortable asking questions of and expressing opinions and concerns to a relative stranger than to close relatives. Of course you will need to be clear with the advisor about what information you do or do not want shared, but as a part of the money mentoring team, this person can help your child come to grips with the larger experience of family affluence with less trauma than if she has to figure things out on her own.

If you take time to give them practice, structure, information, and mentors throughout their early years, you can raise visionaries who have the tools and experience to realize their visions, caretakers who can nurture the family legacy, and self-reliant individuals who can manifest their own deep desires. Guiding your kids in the realm of family finances will give them support on their life journey, helping them transcend money for its own sake and connect to the energy and possibilities of what their wealth can bring them.

"Service is
the rent we pay
for living."

MARIAN WRIGHT EDELMAN,
FOUNDER AND PRESIDENT OF THE
CHILDREN'S DEFENSE FUND

Raising Young Philanthropists

Thomas Jefferson said: "I deem it the duty of every man to devote a certain portion of his income for charitable purposes and that it is his further duty to see it so applied as to do the most good of which it is capable. This I believe to be best insured by keeping within the circle of his own inquiry and information the subjects of distress to whose relief his contributions shall be applied."

David Ben-Gurion, the first prime minister of Israel, said: "The activities of the state of Israel will not be guided solely by economic and political considerations. We would be untrue to ourselves if we ignore the great moral inheritance of our prophets and sages. In that inheritance we inherit the social and humane visions of brotherhood, social justice, and freedom. The state of Israel will be judged, ultimately by the loyalty to the sublime dictate of Judaism: 'Thou shalt love thy neighbor as thyself.' "

Both men, historically over a century apart, were acknowledging that what makes countries (and communities of all sizes) work are the mitigating factors of reciprocity, caring, and concern for the whole community, not just portions of it. Capital markets and political considerations alone will not serve the population's needs for security and well-being.

An estimated 83.9 million American adults formally volunteered roughly 15.5 billion hours in 2000: 62 percent of those people were women. What are your children prepared to give back?

Families are loath to speak to outsiders about their own children's shortcomings. But I am struck by how often mothers, grandparents, aunts, godparents, and close family friends approach me and, in quiet whispers, describe a child who they feel is excessively self-absorbed, disconnected from the needs of others, and seemingly obsessed by the popular culture and the things the culture hawks as desirable. With despair, as though it is a futile quest, they ask if there is anything they can do that will result in a less mall-focused kid.

I often reply that philanthropic activity is one path that can help kids see beyond the doors of Abercrombie & Fitch. Throughout this book I return over and over to the idea that raising a financially fit kid is not just about teaching the skills to build and shepherd assets. At the heart of the exercise is the hope that children will grow up to be aware of and empathic toward people and events outside themselves—which includes being connected to a deeper purpose for their own lives than mere accumulation and consumption.

Young Role Models

I have referred earlier to the work of the Slavitt kids with their Keys to Hope, Craig Kielburger's Kids Can Free the Children, and Samantha Smith's Waging Peace effort. There are also a number of excellent organizations created and managed by adults that offer opportunities for the involvement of young people in some form of philanthropic purpose. But what I appreciate about programs started and led by kids is that they emerge directly from the kids themselves. Their efforts take root because they are an act of mastery for kids, a means of showing competency and caring at the same time. Often they are helped along by caring adults who take the kids' good-hearted impulses seriously and help them act on those impulses—but don't take over the programs. Leaving kids to learn, achieve, make their own mistakes, and make a difference directly is one of the most confidence-building gifts adults can give young people.

> **Philanthropic Initiatives by Young People**
> www.freethechildren.org
> www.freebytes.org
> www.kidsface.org
> www.penniestoprotect policedogs.org
> www.trhf.org
> www.wagingpeace.org

One of my favorite stories in this regard comes from the Humane Society newsletter of California's Santa Clara Valley. Thomas and Andrew Smith (8 and 10, respectively) and neighbor Sean Scanlon (7) held a garage sale in their Los Altos neighborhood with all proceeds benefiting the Humane Society. They organized the sale by collecting used toys, children's books, puzzles, games, and stuffed animals from neighbors in the surrounding cul-de-sacs. The morning of the sale the boys were up early sorting and pricing items and posting garage-sale signs.

"I was really surprised at how much money we made," says Sean. "At first, I wasn't too sure about donating all the money to the Humane Society," says Andrew. "But when we told everyone what the sale was for, people were really excited about it. It made me feel good because I really like animals a lot. And the people who bought things were really nice. They gave extra change or even an extra dollar because they like animals, too."

The Humane Society was unaware of the boys' efforts until one of the moms called for their address so she could send them a check for $241.16. "My mom was really happy, too," said Thomas. "My brother and I finally cleaned up our rooms!"

Encouraging the Generous Impulse

If your kids have not yet shown a readiness to act on the Golden Rule or exercise reciprocity, there are ways to help them exercise that philanthropic muscle and master yet another of the Ten Basic Money Skills.

For the child who has yet to understand that we each hold a sacred obligation to give back, make a contribution, do our share, and love our neighbors as ourselves, drastic action may be demanded. Instead of enduring shouting matches, turning yourself into a most unattractive martyr, or using your good energy to become a constant nag, helping your kids "turn on" their philanthropic instincts is probably a more satisfying course of action.

Philanthropy is as individual as a thumbprint, and exposing young people to the variety of ways in which they can be engaged in philanthropy (as opposed to simply giving money away) is a way of showing them a larger world, offering them an expanded menu of options with which they can explore the world and their place in it. Here are a few of the items on that menu:

Volunteerism: in schools, hospitals, museums, shelters

Charity: giving money, goods, or services to the less fortunate

Social enterprise: businesses and nonprofits whose missions serve a dual purpose of making money and making a difference (self-sustaining contributions, as it were)

Faith-based social services: from the saintly good works of Mother Teresa to the social services of the Salvation Army

Social activism and advocacy: the underpaid, underappreciated efforts of the few to mitigate the harm of the many

Research: learning with a purpose aimed at advocacy, change, education, and advances in the quality of life

Of course, telling children they need to relinquish a part of their allowance to give away to someone else may not be as instantly satisfying as you think it ought to be. As with so many things that are really good for kids, you may need to play a little Tom Sawyer so they can uncover this wisdom for themselves.

By making sure kids are philanthropically oriented you can give them vehicles for achieving connectedness with their community—local and global.

How can you connect your kids to these higher pursuits if their social calendars are filled with parties, time hanging with friends, sports, schoolwork, part-time jobs, and music classes? Piggybacking on the things they already care about is a good way to avoid their knee-jerk instincts to resist your sage advice. Here are a few suggestions:

- Offer to buy an agreed-upon number of CDs for your kid if part of the purchase price of the CD is connected to a cause he cares about.
- Offer to take your kid to one benefit concert or benefit film screening if (1) she can tell you which current performance or film has the most meaning to her and why, and (2) she will donate four hours of her own time to the same cause the entertainers are contributing to.
- Offer to match a donation to a cause your kid chooses if he can make a case for why the cause is important. You may not like his choice, but if he can defend it, you should respect it—unless it's supporting gunrunners in rogue states, of course!
- If you have the resources, offer to fund a summer trip that is fun and gives your kid a chance to give back. Let her know that can mean working in an orphanage in Russia, visiting a kibbutz, working on an archaeological dig site, helping to plant gardens in inner-city neighborhoods, helping Habitat for Humanity build a house, or whatever your child's imagination and a search on the Web can conjure up. Spas, tennis camps, and a month to learn Italian in Tuscany could well be life-enhancing but probably don't fall into the spirit of giving back. Fund challenge and contribution, not luxury.
- Take your child with you on a weekend retreat to a monastery or other reflective locale. (If a weekend is too long, try a day.) The idea is to expose your kid to an environment that gives him a taste of a time-out from everyday consumer life. He may complain that he's bored, but he will remember quiet time spent with you.

- As discussed earlier in the book, engaging your child's peers as your allies is often an effective way to put their power to work for you. Find a local family foundation or kid-run organization based in your community and introduce your child to same-age kids who have begun to explore the possibilities of philanthropy—you'll greatly accelerate your child's learning and awareness process.
- Take your child with you to a philanthropy conference or workshop.
- Introduce a vocabulary of giving (see sidebar).

A Glossary of Philanthropy

Send your kids in search of the meanings for the following terms (feel free to add your own to this list). Offer to give $1 to the charity of their choice for each term learned.

Charity

Grassroots

Development

Philanthropy

Challenge grant

Discretionary funds

Donor

Donee

Endowment

Grant

Pledge

Site visit

RFP

Social entrepreneur

Trust / Trustee

Whether your approach to philanthropy is religious, philosophical, or purely pragmatic, by making sure kids are philanthropically oriented you can give them vehicles for achieving connectedness with their community—local and global. The nurturing of a philanthropic spirit can start very young. When your child puts pennies in Salvation Army kettles at Christmas, goes with you to drop off canned goods at the local homeless shelter, or sets aside part of her allowance each week for a cause she supports, she begins to build a consciousness of sharing that will last well beyond her financial apprenticeship.

In chapter 2 I described the concept of a Charity Café night as a means of engaging young people in a peer activity that offers an alternative to hanging out at the mall and spending money (see page 36 for instructions for establishing a Charity Café). But kids who do get bitten by the excitement of raising and giving money away often find the process is much more complex than they thought. It's one thing to drop clothes off at Goodwill and call it tax deduction, quite another to connect one's life passion with a mission to make a difference or even to pragmatically assess who will use donated money in the most effective ways.

The chart below offers a structure for helping your kids connect the issues they care about with making a real difference for others. After listing the issues or causes that matter most to them (this can be done with kids 9 to 18+), they will see what their instincts for allocating money to these causes tell them about their own priorities. See the following page for specific instructions.

Category	Organization	Amount of Time	Amount of Money	Heart Score
Health				
Animal Issues				
Environment				
Social Justice / Human Rights				
Arts and Education				
Sports				
Other				

a. For each category, fill in the name(s) of one or more organization offering opportunities for change or involvement.

b. Using six hours each week to donate to one or more of the organizations listed, allocate your time.

c. Using $10,000 to give away over a twelve-month period to one or more of the organizations you listed, allocate your money.

d. On a scale of 1 to 10, 1 equaling a cold heart and 10 equaling a heart full of care, rate the concern you have for each of the organizations or issues you have listed.

e. Now take a close look at the chart: are the heart score, the way money was allocated, and the way time was allocated all in sync?

Once a clear picture of what matters to your child begins to emerge, it will be easier to actually *do* something that matters to the young person. Encourage him to look into a range of local programs that match his interests— call or write for materials on each organization, and if his interest grows strong enough, visit the programs with him.

Philanthropy provides a tool for galvanizing kids to master the other nine Basic Money Skills; it also offers an antidote to a mass culture that places far too much value on consuming and accumulating things and money for image and status. Encouraging philanthropic engagement early on can play a critical role in helping kids develop strong values and a sense of purpose and meaning. Kids who feel they are making a difference, that they are part of something greater than themselves, will become more grounded, self-confident adults. Wherever your kids' passions happen to lie, feeling a moral imperative that connects their own interests and privileges to the needs of others will give them a greater sense of community and connectedness in their lives.

Philanthropy Resources

The Giving Family: Raising Our Children to Help Others,
Susan Crites Price (available through the Council on Foundations, www.cof.org)

Inspired Philanthropy: Your Step-by-Step Guide to Creating a Giving Plan,
Tracy Gary and Melissa Kohner

Volunteer Vacations: Short-Term Vacations that Will Benefit You and Others,
Bill McMillon

The Measure of Our Success: A Letter to My Children and Yours,
Marian Wright Edelman

Online resource for family volunteering projects: www.familycares.org

Kids Care Clubs: www.kidscare.org

The Foundation Center: www.fdncenter.org

The Virtual Foundation: www.virtualfoundation.org

Network for Good: www.networkforgood.org

Youth NOISE: www.youthnoise.com

"You can't expect to make a place in the sun for yourself if you keep taking refuge under the family tree."

CLAUDE MCDONALD

Yikes! My Kid Won't Leave Home! Now What?

Not too long ago I ran a workshop on kids and money for the employees of a well-known financial services firm. There were about 150 people in the audience: parents, aunts, uncles, kids' mentors, grandparents, and investment advisors who wanted tips to share with their clients. In other words, a pretty mixed group of people. On this occasion I decided to open the session by asking the audience to share some of their most pressing concerns about kids and money.

The usual list cropped up: how to get kids to care about something more than spending money; how best to encourage philanthropy among the young; when to start and how to manage an allowance; how to support kids who exhibit entrepreneurial urges at an early age. But the one that surprised me in its frequency was this: "My son or daughter is (19, 20, 23, 24) and still living at home. I had expected my children to be launched and on their own by now. My spouse and I are concerned about being able to afford our own retirement and we also have to provide more care for our own parents than we had anticipated. What can I do to help my kid become independent?"

It turns out that a lot of families are harboring children who will not leave the nest. One college freshman told me recently, "The last time I was home on break I sat in my parents' hot tub and thought, 'Damn, this is nice. How am I going to afford this on my own?' I'm not eager to leave there." And truth be told, lots of parents communicate, "There's no reason you should, honey." But there is a very good reason.

Delayed independence often turns into chronic dependence. Developmentally, children begin to test and explore independence as pre-teens. With support and encouragement, most children will successfully make the transition from child to young adult by the time they are ready for college or a full-time job—generally by 18 or 19. Gradually they will spend less and less time at home and more exploring the world. Summer camps, travel with friends, college dorms, and summer jobs out of state all provide opportunities to practice independent living.

And these are the experiences that allow parents to promote independence as well. If you have helped your daughter through a bad bout of homesickness at camp by encouraging her to get through the process rather than come home immediately, or if you have insisted that your son acquire job experience in the summer, chances are you will not be struggling with how to encourage independence in your twentysomething children.

Reasons for Not Leaving Home

There are three big reasons kids get stuck between financial dependence and financial independence and have a hard time leaving home:

1. There are too many incentives to maintain a comfortable status quo (hot tubs, good food, cheap room service). Why leave home when all the amenities are so readily available? And if college life has been equally upscale (many of today's colleges compete for students by offering an array of benefits—from boutique food cafés to wireless connections in dorm rooms—that make taking an extra year or two to complete a four-year program very attractive), adult children who have become accustomed to a certain quality of life may be loath to give it up.

2. Fear, debt, and lack of planning are such that making the move out of the nest seems overwhelming. Kids who have not had a proper financial apprenticeship and see no way of attaining their parents' lifestyle will linger longer to enjoy what they fear they cannot replace.

3. Necessity. The young person's income is necessary to the household, or an illness or other family situation makes his presence vital to the family. In this case, the short-term, everyday needs of the family keep the young person at home—often to the longer-term detriment of the family. A young person pushed to become educated and financially independent can be a lot more helpful than the child who stays at home.

Helping Kids Become Adults

So what can you do if your daughter hasn't found a job she likes and has decided that life at home suits her until she does? What if your son has changed jobs multiple times and is now unemployed and has so much debt on his credit card he can't afford to rent an apartment? What can you do that isn't cruel and cold-hearted?

Probably nothing. That is, nothing that won't *feel* cold-hearted and cruel. Sometimes the best way to get a bird to fly is to nudge it out of the nest—and that takes a very strong form of love. But if you're ready (or just desperate—that works too!), here are a few of the things you can do to help a delayed adolescent transform into an independent adult.

Remember whom you're dealing with. Keep in mind that developmentally you are dealing with an adolescent—not the chronological adult you see in front of you. Use that information to help you stay sane and to guide your own expectations and goals. Basically, you are going to replay the financial apprenticeship from the beginning at warp speed.

It may be a bit shocking for your twentysomething to discover the new tough parent living in the house, but the only way to change the status quo may be to change yourself.

> The more dollars adult children receive, the fewer they accumulate, while those who are given fewer dollars accumulate more.

End subsidies. Even if you can well afford to subsidize your kids, it isn't a good idea. Thomas Stanley and William Danko, authors of *The Millionaire Next Door*—a study of the consumption and spending habits of the affluent—describe parents who subsidize their kids as providing "economic outpatient care." In their research they found that "the more dollars adult children receive, the fewer they accumulate, while those who are given fewer dollars accumulate more."

One of the most astute observations they made in their work was that parents who noticed independent, achievement-oriented behavior in their kids often tended to nurture and encourage those traits, providing opportunities for those kids to be independent. These same parents would then spend more time with the less resourceful children in the family, helping them make decisions—or, worse, making decisions for them. The result of this duality was to "strengthen the strong and weaken the weak." If your aim is to strengthen your kids, you have to give all of them a chance to be strong—even in the face of defiance or fear, which are normal responses to the kind of challenges they're facing.

Charge rent, or help your adult child purchase a condo or small house if that's an option. But don't sign the lease for her and don't arrange the mortgage for her—that's part of the process. One dad told me of his thirtysomething daughter who liked staying at home because "she didn't feel confident she could do anything by herself," as he put it. After I worked with him for a while, I understood that he rarely *expected* her to do anything for herself.

In a way, she had prolonged her experience of being "daddy's little girl" by maintaining a lifestyle of helplessness. Though this had on some level worked for this father for a while, he was now facing retirement and was concerned that his daughter might never be able to take care of herself. The young woman was educated and talented, and worked regularly, but never at a job up to her capacity—or using her graduate education.

Finally, with encouragement from her father, she began to look for a home of her own. It didn't take her long to locate a condo that she liked and that she could, with careful budgeting, maintain on her own. She came home and told her dad about the house. The only catch was that she didn't have enough saved for the down payment.

This time her dad was prepared. He sent her to www.fanniemae.com and told her he would loan her money for a down payment if it became necessary, but that she needed to go through the loan process on her own. Three months later, the daughter had mastered the process of getting her first mortgage and had moved into her new home. Dad had loaned her some of the money for the down payment, but he had demanded a contract between them. He reported to me that he had never seen his daughter so energized or self-confident.

Giving kids opportunities to master the skills of independence is critical to their self-esteem. In the '80s, when self-esteem was first identified as a desirable quality for kids to possess, this concept was accompanied by a misguided notion that just telling kids they were great was all that was needed. All over the world, parents and educators were finding ways to award gold stars with no concomitant expectation except being "a great person."

Happily, that naïveté has passed, and now we know that self-esteem must be earned. Parents who care about helping their child feel internally strong need to make sure they are not helping him avoid facing the challenges that will help him become a competent, self-confident person.

Make a plan with (or without) your child and stick to it. You'll need to set goals and limits that move your child into true adulthood. Is your son in debt? What's the plan to get him out? (No, paying off the debt for him isn't an option.) Give him a time frame and help him figure out how to get out of debt. Maybe he needs to seek out a credit counseling group or take a second job. Your daughter can't afford an apartment that's as nice as her family bedroom? That's reality. Sharing an apartment with a friend or renting a room at the YWCA may be an option. While she's looking for a place, charge rent. She doesn't earn enough at her job to pay you? Fine—does the den need painting? Are you paying for household help? One way or another, you need to help your child make the connection between managing one's money and taking care of oneself.

Push your child out of the house. Set a date by which time he is to be out of the house in an independent living arrangement. You may need to help: how about a summer with an aunt in another state, or a best friend in another country who can be counted upon not to assume a caretaking role? Breaking family habits and living in a fresh environment is another way of encouraging independence.

Be clear, be consistent, be selfish, be calm. Dramatic ultimatums and scenes you can't back down from are generally not very effective. When it comes to helping kids become more independent, negative reinforcement will not achieve the desired goal. If you refocus attention on your self and your own needs, while being clear and consistent about your expectations of and love for your child, you will help her move through this developmental crisis. Being "selfish"—that is, being mindful of your own needs at this stage in your life—may well be the most loving thing you can do for adult children who are afraid to move into full adulthood.

Allow failure, anxiety, and crisis to take their own course. "My son is finally learning life lessons the hard way," one mother confided to me, "and it's killing me." Her son, used to being able to buy what he wanted without being held accountable, was getting overdue exposure to what it means to have no disposable income provided by Mom and Dad and no parental financial safety net. The mother had resolved to let her son experience the summer before he entered college as a kind of homegrown financial boot camp. "Better here near home where the stakes are a little lower," she remarked, "than next fall when he is three thousand miles away and really vulnerable." By refusing to provide economic outpatient care, this mother was giving her son a powerful message that (a) she was going to start treating him like an adult and (b) she respected his ability to function as an adult.

Two truths flutter among the pages of this book. One is that raising kids is complicated work, fraught with the endless psychological, cultural, sociological, and economic variables each family brings to the job. When parents are acting out their own needs through kids or keeping up with the affluent Joneses, or when rebellion in a family is played out through a variety of passive-aggressive tactics, keeping kids on course as they make their way through their financial apprenticeship is no easy task.

The second truth is that if helping your kids become financially responsible is a priority for you, the task is within your reach—and not so very complicated after all. It's always possible to provide good excuses and rational explanations for why your kids aren't moving forward, but with your full commitment, your children can successfully make the transition from their apprenticeship into the next stage of adulthood: Starting Out.

The Ten Basic Money Skills, Take Two

So let's say you've tried everything and your 24-year-old is still living up there under the eaves, eating out of your refrigerator, borrowing your car (and returning it with the tank empty), and expecting you to make another deposit in his or her ATM account—what now?

It's time to take drastic action! When I read W. Bruce Cameron's "8 Simple Rules for Dating My Teenage Daughter," I howled (see www.wbrucecameron.com/pages/columns/8rules.htm). But even as I was giggling, I understood that his rules reflect the real feelings of a desperate parent—the real feelings that lots of dads would post on the front door if they thought it was remotely possible.

Inspired by Cameron's forthright, primal honesty, I decided to create a set of last-ditch rules that can be called on by any parent committed to helping his or her "adult child" leave the nest.

We now move on to *The Ten Basic Money Skills, Take Two*.

Copy the rules on pages 198–199 and hand them to your adult children. With these rules they will develop fiscal fitness very quickly. They may say bad things about you to your grandchildren, but at least those grandchildren will not be living under your roof.

The Ten Basic Money Skills, Take Two

1 As Bill Cosby, playing America's Favorite Dad, put it in an episode of *The Cosby Show:* "Your mother and I have money. You are poor. You must get a job to have money." Therefore, you will get a job—any job—within two weeks, or by the end of the month, whichever comes first. Yes, it may feel unfair—even tragic—for someone of your talents and intellect to squander his gifts so cavalierly by restocking light bulbs at Home Depot or hauling around five-gallon Sparkletts water bottles on your back, especially if someone you know from high school happens to see you in your uniform. But you'd be surprised how many corporate Big Shots got their foot in the door by taking exactly this career path.

2 You will shift your spending and savings habits so radically that the Cineplex, Dominos, The Gap, and Blockbuster Video will notice your absence and the local savings bank will send you a nifty toaster. (And remember, you can sell that toaster on eBay and put the cash back into the savings account. You can always toast bread over a gas burner.)

3 You will find a shelter alternative to the bedroom you've occupied since your 12th birthday. If you don't have enough money for the initial deposit, enlist some of the overeducated ne'er-do-wells who hang around here to join you in a communal living arrangement. Failure to get together enough money for a deposit will leave you with the option of moving into a pup tent in the back yard as your interim housing solution. The advantage of this shelter is that there will be no utility bills to cover, though the long walk to the public bathroom will be inconvenient.

4 As of sundown you will always know your bank balance to the nearest dollar, how much you have spent in the previous seven days (to the penny), and how much, god forbid, you owe. If you cannot reel off this information within fifteen minutes of being asked, you will spend the afternoon rolling the loose penny collection I have been amassing for the last thirty years.

5 When the impulse strikes to part with even the smallest amount of money (except subsistence-level food consumption and bus fare to and from work), you will take a deep breath, just say no, and walk away. You will then consider for twenty-four hours the necessity of making that purchase. If, after that time, you really feel you'll be culturally deprived if you don't get the newest Eminem release, you will figure out a way (like selling a few of the hundreds of other CDs you couldn't live without) to spend only 25 percent of your originally intended outlay.

6 Be prepared to add the subject of finances to those weekly heart-to-heart talks about sex and drugs you and I enjoy so much. There may not be an at-home test for money management, but I do have access to lie-detector technology and I won't be shy about using it.

7 You will live within a budget as if you had no parental unit to bail you out of trouble. You will live this way because from now on, it's true. The only backup you will receive from your parents is a prepaid membership to Overspenders' Anonymous.

8 You will discover the joys of something called an investment portfolio. Once you have the basics under your belt, you will slowly and carefully begin to assemble your own. You will aim for the idea of having a fully diversified portfolio, but you will start off with the purchase of an investment instrument called a Treasury Bill. You can read about T-Bills on the Internet; in fact, you can even purchase them online. Don't get too fond of Internet investing, by the way. If I find you have invested all your savings in a thousand shares of Nobody Has a Clue What We Do Dynamics, I will make you commit the numbers on ten-year note yields for the last six months to memory and recite them for your mother's investment club.

9 You will show curiosity and entrepreneurial initiative, whether you are working for the Post Office or the largest law firm in town. You will do this because coasting through a job is incredibly mind-numbing at best and dehumanizing at worst. You don't want to end up as a disgruntled postal worker, do you?

10 You will not fill out any of the hundreds of preapproved credit-card forms that you receive in the mail until you are 35 and your savings account has more money in it than the cost of a used Hyundai. In the meantime, you can use my credit card in an emergency. An emergency is defined as life-threatening, which is to say, if you use the card for something other than a true emergency, you might consider hari-kari.

Part Four

Map Check

Chapter II
Most Frequently Asked Questions

"You are the
teacher and the taught
and the teaching."

KRISHNAMURTI

Most Frequently
Asked Questions

n case of emergency, you can turn to this last chapter for brief answers to the ten questions I am most frequently asked. If you have solutions that you like better, or questions I haven't addressed, please feel free to email me (contactus@independent means.com) and I'll share your ideas and queries with other parents in the "Raising Financially Fit Kids" newsletter.

Q: Should we start an allowance?

A: Only if you are prepared to live by the Parent's Allowance Mantra: *An allowance is not a salary or an entitlement; it is a tool for learning how to handle money responsibly*. If this works for you, and you can explain your five top money values to your kids, and everyone is clear on how the allowance is to be used, then go for it! For a thorough discussion of allowances, turn to page 54.

Q: Times are tough—how do we teach frugality without causing anxiety?

A: A frequent trigger of anxiety is lack of information. A free-floating worry that "things are not *really* okay" will be a lot more troubling to kids than having a firm grasp on a reality they feel is being dealt with. In other words, include kids in the real issues of your family life—they will often have good ideas to offer and will appreciate being trusted to help out.

Q: How do we help our spendthrift learn to save?

A: First, check out how and why this child has so much disposable income and rework the budget. If she's 16 and working part-time at her Aunt Mae Lee's boutique, but her paychecks are all going toward her wardrobe, and you're still paying for movie tickets, you have a choice: stop subsidizing her behavior. Force some decision making now while the life stakes are not life-threatening.

Q: How do we instill in our little Scrooge the value of sharing with others and giving money to charity?

A: Lead the way. Create a family fund into which everyone puts 5 percent of their income (allowance, birthday gifts, salary). Create a family council to determine where the money accumulated will be contributed each quarter or once a year. Get actively involved with one or two of your donees and make sure that Scrooge has a role in the relationship too. For more information on getting kids involved in philanthropic pursuits, see chapter 9.

Q: How do we compete with the media and the marketing budgets of the nation's largest companies to communicate good financial values to kids?

A: Why do you think those companies have to spend so much money repeating the same messages over and over to your kids? Your kids live with you. These companies have to get past *you* to get to them! You have time and opportunity to inculcate values that will inoculate your kids from the myriad messages they receive every day. Use your advantage and talk with your kids regularly. And make sure you are walking your talk—kids can spot hypocrisy a mile away.

Q: Our kids have trust funds and know we have plenty of money. How do we realistically teach them to save and conserve?

A: Following the wisdom of Bill Cosby in an episode of *The Cosby Show*, this is your money, not be to confused with your children's money. Let your kids know that until they demonstrate they can create their own wealth or add to yours, they will not be written into your will. Then turn to chapter 8 in this book for more on the subject.

Q: How do we help our 24-year-old, who is still living with us, become independent?

A: Stop providing "economic outpatient care." Check out your own behavior and audit the ways in which you are helping young Jean or Joe stay dependent. See chapter 10 for some specific suggestions on how to nudge your kids out of the nest.

Q: My husband and I disagree on how to teach financial responsibility to our kids. What can we do?

A: Nothing. Giving kids conflicting messages about spending, saving, earning, and giving money away is like trying to teach them to speak French while you speak German and your spouse converses in Spanish. Spend some time with your spouse to devise at least a core set of values that you can be in concert on. Then bring in a money mentoring team that can bolster the values you both agree on.

Q: My child is in crisis (Attention Deficit Disorder, poor grades, or acting out). It's all I can do to get her through a day and keep her out of trouble. How am I ever going to teach her fiscal fitness?

A: Use the Ten Basic Money Skills as a solution to her other problems, not as an additional task to take on. Bad behavior? Shift the focus to how she will achieve independence using these skills. Poor grades? A child engaged in experientially learning any of the Ten Basic Money Skills may become more engaged generally (starting a money book club is one way to improve reading skills—see page 36 for tips). Money has the power to focus attention like few other things. Paul Orfela, the founder of Kinko's, is famously ADD and credits his affliction with helping him start the ever-so-successful copy chain. (See *Succeeding with LD* by Jill Lauren for stories of twenty people who triumphed with learning differences.)

Q: I don't want my kids to think about money all the time. Why should I introduce the subject when they are so young?

A: Financial literacy is not just about the money. It's about launching great kids: giving them the skills and knowledge to take care of themselves and to be contributing members of both their family and their community. It's about helping them create their own personal financial safety nets. Financial literacy is economic self-defense. Start early to arm your kids well.

Index